GAMES FOR SOCIAL AND LIFE SKILLS

Games for Social and Life Skills

Tim Bond

Stanley Thornes (Publishers) Ltd

First published in 1986 by Hutchinson Education

Reprinted 1990 by
Stanley Thornes (Publishers) Ltd
Ellenborough House
Wellington Street
CHELTENHAM GL50 1YW
England

97 98 99 00 / 10 9 8

British Library Cataloguing in Publication Data
Bond, Tim
    Games for social and life skills.
    1. Life skills–Study and teaching (Secondary)
    2. Education games
    I. Title
    320'07'12   LC268

ISBN 0 7487 0339 X

Set in VIP Rockwell by D.P. Media Ltd
Printed and bound in Great Britain at SRP Ltd, Exeter

Contents

Acknowledgements

Thanks to

all my students who willingly participated in trial runs of the games and especially Denise Priest who drew the cat illustrated in L1 **The owl and the pussycat**. I am also grateful to those supervisors working on the Youth Training Scheme and the social workers who tried out games and suggested improvements.

My thanks also go to friends and colleagues who encouraged the writing of this book or helped with revising the script, especially Terry Dunphy, Staff Tutor of the Durham Accredited Training Centre, Alan Perks, Head of Drama and Deputy House Head at Harwich Comprehensive School, Steve Bolam, Clive Constance, Linda McKie, Jan Race, Albert Toal, Chris White, the Neville's Cross Centre Library Staff at New College, Durham, Denise Punton who typed the script and many others.

Many of the ideas for games included in the book were the creation of unknown minds and have reached me only by word of mouth. My thanks to you. I hope you feel that the way I have adapted them for this book does them justice.

Biographical note

Tim Bond, B A, C Q S W, Cert. Ed. has worked as a social worker in a variety of settings before he became interested in education and training as a means of helping people to realize their full potential. He is currently employed as a college counsellor and senior lecturer. He enjoys this opportunity to combine practice with training others, a combination which has informed the development of this book.

His original intention was to produce a short handout for his students involved in social and life skills training. Although the writing prospered during the hot summer of 1984 he saw very little of the sunshine as the project grew. He was comforted by the thought that the book would outlive the suntans. His dog, Gertie, was less easily consoled.

INTRODUCTION

LEARNING THROUGH GAMES

Games are fun and this makes them an enjoyable way of learning. There is nothing unusual in games serving ends in addition to those of exercise and fun. When children play at being parents they are coming to terms with their own family life and rehearsing adult roles as well as having fun. There is no good reason why such a universal method of learning in childhood should not continue into adult life. Young people and adults still retain an interest in leisure activities. This enthusiasm for fun and friendship can be tapped for teaching social skills – in the widest sense of that phrase.

As games offer the participants structured experiences they are particularly suitable for improving social skills. The structure of the game can focus the experience on specific issues. In addition, learning by direct personal experience has far more impact than being advised on the basis of someone else's experience, which is inevitably second-hand. First-hand experience makes it easier for someone to relate to whatever they have learnt from the game and to apply it to everyday life.

Games are an exciting and rewarding method of social education because of the way they use the social interactions within groups. This means that responsibility for the outcome of the game does not rest entirely on the facilitator's shoulders but is a responsibility shared with the participants and is in itself a valuable experience. Games build on the energy of informal interactions rather than repress them in the ways more rigid methods of learning require. Since the dynamics of each group interaction is different, every time the same game is used there will be variations. Running games, like other ways of using interpersonal skills, can become a long-term interest, the facilitator acquiring considerable skills. But they can also be used with reasonable success by a complete beginner.

All the games in this book have been selected because of their proven usefulness with young people and adults. I hope other people will have as much productive fun with them as I have had in presenting and testing them.

Invitation to comment on the games and suggest new ones
All games users quickly learn how to adapt games to their own needs, and

sometimes wholly new games or important variations grow out of this process. I would be interested in hearing about these or any useful games not included in the book. Details of the origins of the games or how they were discovered would be appreciated. They will not be published without acknowledgement.

All letters should be addressed to Tim Bond, Ideas for Games, c/o Stanley Thornes (Publishers) Ltd at the address given on page 4.

THE ADVANTAGES OF GAMES

1 **Motivation**
The association of the word 'games' with fun and friendship ensures that many groups will use this form of learning with enthusiasm. If a group is particularly self-conscious for any reason, then following the instructions in the section **Encouraging participation** will help to overcome this.

2 **Safe environment**
Social and life skills cannot easily be passed on without the opportunities to practise them. Games provide a safe environment in which to do this. They allow group members to experiment with new behaviour and to make errors without incurring the costs of similar mistakes in real life.

3 **People can change**
Games are one way of conveying the message that everyone can choose to change themselves or their relationships with others. Games by themselves are unlikely to change long-term or more intractable problems but they can motivate participants to seek help from counsellors or elsewhere. Games used correctly can support this process and are often sufficient to effect some changes or to begin the process of personal change if the participant wants this.

4 **Involvement**
Games encourage the participation of the less expressive and less dominant group members. Typically everyone has a role in the game and either by the structure of small group discussions or because of involvement in the activity a greater number of people become involved in the discussion afterwards. The discussion is usually more exciting for the participants because it grows out of an activity.

5 **Taking responsibility**
Games provide a structure which can be used to reduce dependency on the leader as the one who is all powerful or who 'knows it all'. The

participants are forced to accept some responsibility for making their part of the activities work, especially if a democratic style of leadership is adopted. In this way games can encourage self-reliance and improve self-confidence.

6 **Flexibility and relevance**
Because the participants contribute their own experiences and skills, and the rules encourage this to happen, each group uses the game at its own level and in its own way. This input by the group also helps to ensure that the game seems relevant to the participants. It is surprising to see how differently each group uses the same game.

7 **Receptiveness**
Because games take place in an atmosphere of fun and the levels of anxiety remain relatively low, people do not feel defensive. This means they are more likely to hear what is said and to be able to evaluate it for themselves. The heightened emotions that are produced by anxiety create selective hearing or even a total inability to hear what is said.

8 **Group cohesiveness**
Games encourage cohesiveness in the group and a sense of group identity. This is particularly true if the games selected encourage cooperation and improved communication in the group.

9 **Framework and structure**
Games offer a framework and structure to group experiences which allow leaders to work within their own limitations of experience and skill by selecting appropriate games. They also open up the possibility of offering group experiences led by people who would not feel at ease in an unstructured group. However, this does not mean games are leader-proofed against all possible blunders nor should they be run without preparation or the opportunity for some kind of supervision. They are an effective method of achieving rapid learning within a task-orientated setting and this process can be considerably helped or hindered by the leader.

USING A GAME FOR THE FIRST TIME

Many people, regardless of previous experience, find it helpful when they are using a game for the first time to have a 'dummy run' on colleagues or friends. This allows the leader to become familiar with the procedures and any hidden snags. If the game needs to be adapted for a particular purpose these changes can be tried at the same time. Its greatest value is the opportunity to test out a variety of strategies and interventions and to receive comments on their usefulness.

After running the game through all its stages you can use these questions to structure the feedback:

- How does the trial group feel now?
- What did they enjoy or find useful?
- Could the leader do anything to improve participation within the game?
- How does this trial group differ from the group the game is intended for?
- How will their responses differ from the trial group?

This kind of discussion will involve you in receiving feedback about your contribution to the dummy run. This can take real courage and self-confidence to discuss it so openly. If for any reason you cannot discuss these matters with the whole group then they can be taken up with one or two trusted members of the trial group afterwards. This is an important process not only in running a game but also for the development of the leader's self-awareness and receptiveness to feedback.

Feedback may not be offered in quite the same way in a game but a leader should be able to receive feedback in a considered and open way. Exposing oneself to feedback is not always comfortable especially if this has not been part of your previous training. It becomes a more familiar and a less threatening process with repetition. However, if you feel totally unable to expose yourself to constructive feedback then games are probably not an appropriate method for you.

Value of joint leadership
Other good ways to learn are to work alongside a more experienced person when they are running a game or to share the leadership with someone you trust. Each person's role can be reviewed after the game.

PREPARING TO RUN GAMES

Games should not be undertaken too lightly. Careful preparation is required if they are to succeed. The most obvious factors are the practical ones of time, place and materials as well as selecting a game that is appropriate to the participants.

However, it is equally important that you prepare yourself mentally and emotionally so that you can encourage the kind of participation that makes the most of the personal energy the game releases. Some games do involve looking at other people's opinions of us and this is a sensitive area which requires careful handling. Many people prefer the discomforts of remaining as they are rather than risk greater self-knowledge and moving into a less familiar world. You as the leader can do a great deal which will support this process of change and assist the development of appropriate social skills.

PRACTICAL MATTERS

All the games included in this book require only modest resources.

1 **Accommodation**

This needs to provide sufficient space for the planned activity. If there are any special requirements these are clearly stated in the instructions.

Choose rooms where participants can make a noise. If you have to keep asking them to do or discuss something quietly this will inhibit their enjoyment and ability to use the game in a way which seems relevant to them.

2 **Materials**

Where these are required they are clearly indicated at the start of each game and in the introduction to each section.

3 **Group size**

This may be important as there are not many games suitable for very small groups. The group sizes indicated in the table at the beginning of each section are no more than a rough guide for the first few runs through. Numbers of participants can vary considerably unless otherwise stated in the instructions. Larger groups can be split up so that there are several groups all playing the same game. The important factor is deciding how many people you feel you can cope with comfortably.

4 **Time available**

There must be enough time for both the activity and the discussion. It is sometimes tempting to compress the discussion but if this happens much of the usefulness of the game is lost. The times indicated for each game are the average of several runs through the game. They are useful for the first few runs through until you find out whether your groups are generally quicker or slower.

5 **Age range**

All the games have been written with both young people and adults in mind. They have been designed to allow different groups to concentrate on their own particular needs and interests. Different groups of the same age range will use the same game in very different ways. Be prepared to be flexible.

6 **Ability of the group**

The games that are used should be within the ability range of the group. Some of the games have been successfully used with handicapped people whereas others are obviously unsuitable because they demand more mobility or movement than is possible. A more frequently encountered limitation is a group with few reading or writing skills. If the game is based on spoken instructions only, there is no problem. Some games are presented in a way which also includes written instructions to cope with complex rules. This does not mean that these instructions could not be given in spoken form. However, giving them this way often requires great patience and a willingness to repeat them on demand with good humour, if the participants are to retain the same sense of security they would have had if they had been able to use written instructions.

ENCOURAGING PARTICIPATION

The emotional climate during a game is crucial to its success. The aim is to create an atmosphere which encourages both maximum participation and the use of the game in a way which is particularly rewarding.

1 Sense of fun

If you can keep a sense of fun at the beginning of the game it helps to get it going and encourages maximum involvement.

The level of fun may rise and fall during a game and may change to absorbed interest as people become more involved. Only if the fun is carried too far or goes on too long do you need to worry about it obscuring the value of the game. Instead of intervening to stop the excessively high spirits you can hold back and include it as an issue in the discussion later.

2 Building trust

A trusting atmosphere allows people to take risks and to reveal more of themselves. Like fun it creates an atmosphere where it is easier to listen to other people's opinions of us without trying to deny them. It also reduces the threat of increased self-awareness which is the basis of improving social skills. There are several ways you can help to encourage trust.

a Establishing ground rules

These remove some of the major uncertainties of participating in a game by establishing an agreement between the participants. This can be formally acknowledged either by voting on them or by everyone saying, 'Agreed.' It is recommended that the rules include:

i That everyone accepts personal responsibility for trying to use the game for self-development. This may be either an internal process or something which can be shared with the group. The more they put into the game the more they get out of it.

ii That on the other hand no one will be required to reveal things about themselves they do not wish to. Everyone should feel able to say, 'This is too personal for me to talk about just now.' If this is said honestly it is not a cop-out, and it may be that it can be shared later on or with a different set of people. Follow-up studies of some of the games have shown that sometimes people seem withdrawn because something has made a considerable impact on them rather than because of indifference to what is happening. Experience enables the leader to spot this happening.

iii That anyone who is still puzzled or worried about something after the game may discuss it with the leader afterwards.

iv That everything said in the game is kept confidential and discussed only within the group. This avoids the danger of some people not participating because they are afraid of being gossiped about.

A few games have twists in them and it would make them difficult to use in the same place again if they were discussed outside the group.

Ground rules are usually best established after the introductions or after a warm-up. If they are used as the very first activity it suggests that what is about to follow will be frightening. If the ground rules are discussed after the group has lost its initial strangeness they help to establish trust.

b *Avoiding exclusion games*

None of the games in this book involve someone being singled out as a loser or being sent away from the group so that something can be planned behind their back. These sorts of games often break down the atmosphere of trust.

c *Giving feedback*

This is an important social skill not only for the leader but also for the participants. The way you offer criticism or give feedback as the leader will influence the group members and work for greater trust.

Feedback is most useful if it is specific and it describes actual behaviour in some detail, e.g. to say 'You are friendly' is less useful than describing the actual behaviour such as smiling or laughing with people.

It is important that it is about something within the control of the listener, e.g. the way they speak, but not about moles on the nose.

It is easiest to accept feedback when it is phrased positively. 'I like you best when you . . .' or 'You could get on better with this group if . . .' creates the hope that change will be emotionally rewarding.

Unspecific general negative criticism, e.g. 'You are useless', or 'You are never any good', should be avoided. It is emotionally devastating and leaves the listener uncertain of what to do to improve. If group members use this type of criticism they should be asked to practise giving feedback in a positive and specific way.

All feedback is at its most effective when it is given at the request of the recipient.

If feedback is used appropriately in everyday life it is one of the social skills which promotes good mental health by producing an informed but positive self-image.

d *Receiving feedback*

Receiving feedback can be made more difficult by the heightened feelings it produces in the listener. These emotions increase the likelihood of something being misheard or blocked out altogether. Therefore, it is important to encourage the listener to check out what has been said.

e *Acceptance*

This goes further than just being non-judgemental about what is said. It involves conveying respect for the group members' right to make their own decisions and to build on their own resources and experiences. Acceptance is conveyed as much by actions as by words, e.g. giving someone attention or time whether or not you share the same views.

3 **Participants' feeling valued**

a *Being listened to*

Active listening is something which is much harder to achieve when you are under pressure for any reason. As far as possible you should be adequately prepared so that at least you are not suffering from uncertainties about the game. Even without avoidable pressures it is not easy because your mind will think more quickly than the other person can speak, which makes concentrating on what is said harder.

One of the simplest techniques of showing that you have listened is to repeat back to the speaker a brief summary of what you have heard.

When emotions are running high it is well worth your checking out what has been said because of the way the feelings can cause selective hearing. This can be done either by giving a summary of what has been said or by asking a question, e.g. 'You are sounding upset because of what Dave has said about you opting out. Can I just check what you meant by your reply?' This way of phrasing the question acknowledges the other person's feelings and their cause. This reduces the sense of distance between the speaker and distressed listener who is now more likely to respond to your question in a way which clarifies and adds to what has been said.

b *Democratic style of leadership*
A democratic style of leadership produces the best quality of work. It also ensures that the participants are most likely to own their new skills and insights after the game is finished and then try to apply them to everyday life. It has five important aspects:

i The group is actively involved in any decision making and this process is encouraged by the leader.
ii Group decisions are based on discussion. If the group asks for technical advice the leader suggests more than one alternative. Instruction sheets and quizzes are to be seen as working documents that can be changed to meet the group's wishes. Flexibility by the leader confirms the value of the participant's contribution.
iii Members choose who they are going to work with within the restrictions imposed by the game, e.g. groups of certain size, or pairs of people not previously known to each other.
iv The leader is specific and factual in his praise or criticism and avoids showing personal bias.
v The leader takes part in the activities on equal terms. This is also valuable for other reasons explored later in this section.

The democratic leader is quite distinct from the authoritarian leader who imposes his/her wishes on the group and then remains aloof. It also contrasts with the laissez-faire or 'do what you want' leader who gives the group complete freedom and does not contribute until asked.

4 Leader as model
Participating on equal terms allows you to set the standard for a game. If you are seen to opt out of your turn or to duck difficult issues the group

will feel able to do the same. Your behaviour as the leader becomes the model for the group.

Being the model is also valuable because it allows you to set useful examples of social skills, e.g. giving feedback constructively.

5 **Value the leader's personal qualities**

Although someone using games for the first time can obtain acceptable results, they can be improved by becoming more practised in counselling, group work or social skills training. Some key works in each of these areas are included in the section **Useful books**.

However skilled you become it is important to remember that your ability to help people develop personally with games and other methods is substantially affected by your personal qualities. Your sensitivity to the feelings of others, genuineness, positive regard for others' points of view and a willingness to listen to them will account for at least half of your ability to encourage creative participation. It is as important to develop these qualities as it is to master particular skills or systems of working with groups.

THE STAGES OF A GAME

STAGE	LEADER'S ROLE
1 Introducing the game	- explaining instructions clearly - allocating roles* - referring to the ground rules*
2 Activity	- participating on equal terms - using own participation as a model for others - enabling the group to adapt and develop the game towards their own interests or needs - negotiating changes to planned activity
3 Discussion	- all of above - assisting formation of the discussion groups* - structuring the discussion* - summarizing the discussion - encouraging application of new skills and insights - assisting realistic goal setting - negotiating clear agreement about what the participants will do next
4 Work outside the group *	- encouraging participants on request
5 Reporting back*	- reinforcing successes - reviewing goal setting for non-achievers - encouraging planning for progress
6 Review of your role as leader	- being open to feedback

*Not necessary to all the games.

RUNNING THE GAME

1 **Introducing the game**
  a *Giving instructions*
    These should be given clearly at the beginning of a game with opportunities to ask questions. This will avoid the uncertainties and frustrations which can interrupt the flow of activity once a game is started.

  b *Allocating roles*
    Many of the games require dividing the whole group into smaller parts and then allocating roles. When you are doing this ask a group to divide into groups of the required size and ask them to decide who is A, B and C, etc. The leader then allocates the roles to the particular letters, e.g. 'A is the observer, B is the listener and C is the interviewer.' Groups find this method easier than agreeing specified roles for each other and so the game starts with a greater sense of purpose.

  c *Referring to ground rules*
    It is sometimes helpful to remind the participants of the agreed ground rules to allay any anxiety or to prevent likely breaches.

2 **Activity**
  a *Value of leader's participation*
    Games are not just a way of occupying people while the leader does something else. The way you participate sets the standards of the game. If you opt out or are half-hearted you cannot blame the group members for doing the same. Your involvement in the game increases the acceptability of your interventions in the eyes of the group.

  b *Adapting the game*
    Negotiating changes to the game initiated by the participants increases its relevance to them and is in itself useful experience of a social skill.

  c *Finding topics for discussion*
    Some of the activities are based on the group discussing something

which interests them. Brainstorming is one of the most successful ways of finding topics which interest the group. It involves the leader asking for ideas from the group and then writing them down publicly on a blackboard or flipchart. All the ideas are recorded by the leader without comment from anyone regardless of how good or silly they seem. When the list is completed, or sufficient ideas have been collected, the group is asked to say which seems the most interesting and perhaps to vote on the two or three most popular choices if the exact amount of support is not clear. Near winners can be held in reserve for the next time they are needed. Sometimes ideas which seem silly at first stimulate new thinking on a topic but at other times they just drop out of the running without you having to say anything.

3 **Discussion**
a *The importance of the discussion*
This stage should never be omitted or rushed. The discussion is an important part of experiencing a game. It allows everyone involved in the game to look at their feelings and to come to terms with any that are unresolved. It is an opportunity to further self-awareness as well as practising communication skills. Most importantly discussion is an effective means of motivating personal change.

Research by Lewin showed that discussions were ten times more effective than lectures or talks. About 32% attempted the changes agreed by the group, compared to 3% who attended a lecture encouraging the same changes. Other research produces similar results and repeating the experiment can be a valuable group exercise in itself (see **Useful books**). Lewin explained what happened by comparing the two situations. The lecture is listened to passively with the possibility of resisting the suggested course of action, e.g. 'It might work for the speaker but it won't work for me.' Even if the listeners are considering making a change they cannot be sure of the support of others because the decision is made in social isolation. However, in a group discussion views are exchanged and this process is thought to reduce resistance to change. It is also possible to consider the value of the new ideas by swapping views; whatever is finally decided becomes the group's norm. This sense of group approval helps it to become an internal commitment for each person which continues long after the discussion. This commitment can be increased by making the agreement explicit by voting or by each person expressing their intention. In the games this takes place during the final phase of the discussion during the process of personal goal setting and planning for further action.

b *Phases of the discussion*

Thinking of the discussion as consisting of three phases provides a method of working from feelings through thinking about the game to forming an action plan. Often the phases do not progress as neatly as the diagram suggests. This does not matter but recognizing the phase of the discussion gives you a clue as to how to respond and what to expect from the participants.

PHASE	DESCRIPTION	GROUP LEADER	PARTICIPANTS
ONE	EXPRESSING AND EXPERIENCING FEELINGS	Encourages exploration of feelings about game Is relatively passive	Engage in self-exploration of feelings Experience self more fully Develop insights Attempt self-understanding
TWO	THINKING ABOUT THE GAME	Focusses on thoughts about what happened Is more active	Look at what happened Listen to reports of observers (if any) Compare thoughts about the game Evaluate performance of skills
THREE	PLANNING FURTHER ACTION	Focusses thoughts on life outside the group Assists in establishing realistic goals Encourages a method of reporting progress back to the group/or to group members after the sessions are finished	Consider applications of the game to everyday life Select and plan to satisfy main goals Publicly declare realistic action plan

It is important that the participants are given the opportunity to explore both their feelings and thoughts before proceeding to planning further action. Their feelings are explored first in the spirit of 'how can I know what I feel until I hear what I say?' so they are sufficiently aware of them to be able to use the game to meet their declared needs. It also helps to prevent undisclosed feelings confusing thinking about the game.

The final phase is looking at the implications of the game for experiences and behaviour outside the immediate group of participants. However, as in the earlier stages of the game it is important to be flexible and this structure applies better to some games than to others. Most of the suggested discussions in the book follow this pattern. When the first questions are not about feelings you could let the group talk amongst themselves for a few moments before beginning the discussion. You will probably hear statements like 'That was good/bad' and 'I felt . . .' and other expressions of feelings. If this is not an appropriate method you may wish to ask, 'How do you feel about what you have just done?' before starting the suggested discussion.

Even shy and quiet participants are likely to take part in the discussion because the preceding activity will have broken the ice. Some may still need a specific invitation to say something by directing questions at them, but this will be made less likely the more you are able to encourage participation in the ways described in the previous section.

4 Work outside the group

This can be achieved in many ways, from completing quizzes in the participants' own time, to looking for examples of situations where particular skills could help, or attempting to use them. This helps to identify the games as relevant to everyday life as well as allowing exploration of particular problems which may arise in the transfer of insights and skills from the game to other situations.

5 Reporting back progress

Reporting back gives an opportunity for reinforcing the value of any successes that have been achieved or to re-examine any goals which have proved unrealistic. Both the discussion and this stage carry an important message: 'Personal change is possible if you want it. No one has to remain just as they are for ever. You can choose how you want to change and take control of how you do so.'

Reporting back can be of advantage to the whole group if future meetings are planned. If this is not possible then individual participants can agree to contact one or more of the others to discuss what has happened. These arrangements should be as precise as possible in terms of time and place as this makes the meetings more likely to happen.

6 Reviewing your role as leader

This is the time when you can plan to improve your own skills. It does require a willingness to be open to honest feedback but this can be very valuable and emotionally rewarding.

If you have been running the game(s) with a colleague then an honest discussion with each other including positive specific feedback is probably the best way of conducting the review.

If you have been running the game(s) on your own then discussion with other people who use similar types of experiential learning will prove useful. These discussions might be with one experienced person or in peer groups where you can swap ideas and experiences and set personal goals.

Periodically it is worth reviewing your own overall performance. One of the ways of doing this is to complete your own quiz, working through the skills you consider important.

SKILLS FOR LEADERS OF GAMES – QUIZ

The contents of this self-assessment quiz were suggested by supervisors for the Age Concern Youth Training Scheme in the Durham area. The list is not exhaustive but is the result of the collective experience of ten adults training to use games. It may be used either for self-assessment on one's own or in groups, in which case it can form the basis of a discussion.

Instructions
1   *Read through the whole list.*
2   *Put a circle around the number which represents your current performance. Work through the whole list.*
3   *Place an arrow from the circled number to where you would like to be realistically by the end of this course. Work through the whole list. E.g.*

    1   ②—*3*→*4*   *5*

4   *In the space provided select five skills you would most like to develop during the course.*

Code
1   **Never** *good at that skill.*
2   **Seldom** *good at it.*
3   **Sometimes** *good at it.*
4   **Often** *good at it.*
5   **Always** *good at it.*

Preparation skills
NB. Poor preparation produces poor performance

– planning time	1 2 3 4 5
– planning theme(s)	1 2 3 4 5
– selecting material	1 2 3 4 5
– variety of ideas	1 2 3 4 5
– planning variety of activities	1 2 3 4 5
– choosing appropriate environment	1 2 3 4 5
– checking materials required	1 2 3 4 5

Listening skills
– able to recall and repeat what has been said	1 2 3 4 5
– showing interest by posture	1 2 3 4 5
– able to put own personal feelings from experiences outside the group to one side	1 2 3 4 5

- encouraging others to start speaking   1 2 3 4 5
- using correct names   1 2 3 4 5

Expressing oneself
- clear diction/speech   1 2 3 4 5
- good pace of speech   1 2 3 4 5
- variety of pitch and pace   1 2 3 4 5
- different ways of saying something   1 2 3 4 5
- able to give instructions   1 2 3 4 5
- able to express own ideas   1 2 3 4 5

Responding/intervening
- able to describe own feelings   1 2 3 4 5
- able to clarify other people's ideas   1 2 3 4 5
- able to reflect other people's feelings   1 2 3 4 5
- able to demonstrate what is wanted   1 2 3 4 5
- asking questions   1 2 3 4 5
- confronting   1 2 3 4 5
- giving helpful feedback/criticism   1 2 3 4 5
- receiving criticism/feedback   1 2 3 4 5
- encouraging group participation   1 2 3 4 5
- encouraging group decision making   1 2 3 4 5
- negotiating   1 2 3 4 5
- being flexible   1 2 3 4 5
- unbiased attitude to individuals   1 2 3 4 5
- explore applications to everyday life   1 2 3 4 5

Monitoring/observing
- know who speaks most   1 2 3 4 5
- know who doesn't speak   1 2 3 4 5
- aware of body posture of participants   1 2 3 4 5
- checking out feelings of participants   1 2 3 4 5
- aware of changing relationships in group   1 2 3 4 5

List for the skills you would most like to develop

1 _____

2 _____

3 _____

4 _____

5 _____

THE USE OF GAMES IN SEQUENCE AS PART OF A COURSE OR TRAINING PROGRAMME

Using games in a planned sequence considerably increases their impact. It also increases the probability that all the participants will find something central to themselves in the range of activities. The way the games are classified in the book is to assist in planning sequences of games which build upon each other. It also allows you to use games providing a variety of activities. This is essential to any sustained programme.

1 One of the major uses of games in sequence is the way they can be used to identify and practise social skills in a relaxed environment before gradually working towards the use of skills in everyday life. E.g. dealing with a customer:

IDENTIFY AND FOCUS ON PARTICULAR SKILLS	BRING SKILLS AND PRACTICE TOGETHER	OBSERVED PRACTICE IN THE WORK ENVIRONMENT
Listening * Asking Questions * Explain, Persuade Advise &c.	C1 Predicaments C2 Role Play	Use of new skills at work

*Select games from the appropriate sections.

2 Games can also be used as part of a sequence of different training methods to provide variety in the programme. E.g.

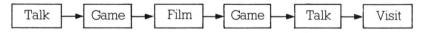

Reinforcing the main points by personal experience makes them much more memorable. Moments of activity help the participants to concentrate in the periods of sitting passively during talks and films, etc.

EXAMPLES OF SHORT COURSES

TWO-DAY COURSE OF SOCIAL AND LIFE SKILLS
Day one – Theme: Looking at oneself

START TIME	TOPIC	GAME/QUIZ	TIME TAKEN
9.00	Introductions	A1 MY NEIGHBOUR IS ... or A2 MIME AN INTEREST or A3 DETECTIVE	30 minutes
9.30	Ground rules		20 minutes
9.50	C O F F E E		10 minutes
10.00	Self-awareness	B6 LABELS C1 PREDICAMENTS	60 minutes 45 minutes
11.45		Ask group to discuss how far what has been said in C1 confirms or disproves B6	15 minutes
12.00	L U N C H		60 minutes
1.00	Needs and planning to satisfy them	D2 DREAM E1 HOUSE OF CARDS or E2 FLYING FAR	30 minutes 45 minutes
2.15	Looking at skills	C5 SOCIAL SKILLS WITH OTHERS	45 minutes
3.00	T E A		15 minutes
3.15	Looking at skills in obtaining work/ or needed at work	C3 THE JOB INTERVIEW or C2 ROLE PLAY OF WORK SITUATION	60 minutes
4.15		Brainstorm skills needed and discuss how to obtain them	15 minutes
HOMEWORK	Looking ahead	F PLANNING WHAT TO DO NEXT	Own time

Day two – Theme: Looking at relating to others

START TIME	TOPIC	GAME/QUIZ		TIME TAKEN
9.00	Review Day 1	Discussion of Day 1 and feedback on homework		20 minutes
9.20	Relationships with others in group in everyday life	G3 or G2	THE MACE THE WHEEL	30 minutes
9.50	C O F F E E			10 minutes
10.00	Skills in relating to others			
	- Listening	H3 H4	LISTENING CHAIN LISTENING IN THREES	30 minutes 30 minutes
11.00	- Asking questions	I2 I5	SHAPES RADIO INTERVIEW	20 minutes 30 minutes
12.00	L U N C H			60 minutes
1.00	Review morning			10 minutes
1.10	- Giving and receiving feedback			
	- needs to be specific	K1	DRAW THIS ...	20 minutes
	- phrased positively	K4	THE MESSAGE OF HAPPINESS	15 minutes
	- practice	K6 or K5	COMPUTER THE BAD AND THE GOOD	40 minutes
2.25	- Sharing, negotiating and compromose	M2	DREAM HOLIDAY	35 minutes
3.00	T E A			15 minutes
3.15	Planning the way ahead	P3	ACHIEVEMENTS	40 minutes
3.55	Ending positively	P1	POSITIVE STROKES	15 minutes
4.10	Goodbyes	P5	REFLECTIONS	20 minutes

APPLYING FOR WORK

Preparation:

Ask the participants to come dressed as they would for a real job interview.

Day one

START TIME	TOPIC	ACTIVITY	TIME TAKEN
9.00	Introduction - selling oneself - speaking clearly	A1 MY NEIGHBOUR IS ... (VARIATION 2)	30 minutes
9.30	Programme and ground rules	Explain programme and ground rules	30 minutes
10.00	C O F F E E		15 minutes
10.15	Choosing a job	Formal input by careers adviser/film	40 minutes
10.55	Looking at the employer's point of view	M3 WORKMATE L3 ESCAPE	70 minutes
		Brainstorm 'what an employer is looking for'	10 minutes
12.15	L U N C H		60 minutes
1.15	Filling job application form	Formal session using real application forms or the specimen form after this section	60 minutes
		Divide into threes and discuss each other's completed forms Large group discussion afterwards	30 minutes
2.45	Preparing for the interview		
	- appearance	K5 THE BAD AND THE GOOD focussed on appearance	15 minutes
3.00	T E A		15 minutes

3.15	Preparing for the interview (cont.)		
	- posture and communication skills	H5 PAYING ATTENTION	45 minutes
4.00	Introduce Homework		15 minutes

WORK IN OWN TIME		1 Select job you would apply for.	Own time
		2 What questions would an employer ask?	
		3 Prepare answers.	

Day two

START TIME	TOPIC	ACTIVITY	TIME TAKEN
9.00	Review	Go over previous day Look at flipchart of what an employer wants	30 minutes
	Selling oneself	Divide into pairs and discuss each other's good points which would attract an employer	30 minutes
10.00	C O F F E E		15 minutes
10.15	Visit by employer(s)	Talk by employer(s) about interviews Questions and answers	45 minutes
11.00	Rehearsal of job interview	C3 THE JOB INTERVIEW or I6 THE JOB INTERVIEW (VARIATION)	80 minutes
12.10	Endgame	P3 ACHIEVEMENTS	20 minutes

Specimen job application form

Mr/Mrs/Miss/Ms   Surname:

Other names:

Previous surname (if appropriate)

Age	Date of birth	Nationality

EDUCATION FROM AGE 11 (School and after school)

School or College	Dates	Examinations taken/ other qualifications	Results

(Specimen job application form cont.)

Give details of any examinations or other course you do not yet have the result for

If in employment give details:

Employer	Dates	Job description

(Specimen job application form cont.)

INTERESTS, e.g. hobbies, sports, voluntary work, youth organizations

Are you related to anyone working for this organization?   YES/NO

If yes, state – name of person . . . .

– relationship . . . .

(Specimen job application form cont.)

Give reasons for wanting this job and any other information which will support this application.

SIGNATURE: .... DATE: ....

THE GAMES

Introducing people to each other

Aims

1 To make people feel at ease in a group of strangers.

2 To create an atmosphere in which people feel able to talk more freely.

General comments

A1 **My neighbour is . . .** encourages listening skills and communication in public but may be familiar to many experienced members of a group who may enjoy the twist in A4 **Truth and deception**.

A2 **Mime an interest** is a good physical warm-up as well as an introduction. A5 **What's my line?** is a gentler introduction and warm-up.

A3 **Detective** works best with a group of people who have different backgrounds and interests.

GAME	TIME	GROUP	MATERIALS
A1 MY NEIGHBOUR IS ...	15 minutes + 2 minutes for each member	To work in pairs	Pens and paper
A2 MIME AN INTEREST	4 minutes for each member approx.	Works better with more than 10	None
A3 DETECTIVE	25 minutes approx.	Capable of dividing into pairs	Pens and paper
A4 TRUTH AND DECEPTION	3-4 minutes for each member	To work in pairs	Instruction sheets
A5 WHAT'S MY LINE?	2-3 minutes for each member	Any number capable of dividing into 5 or 6	None

Other suitable games: C3, I4.

MY NEIGHBOUR IS . . .

Materials: Pens and paper.

Time: 15 minutes + 2 minutes for each member.

Procedure
1 Distribute pens and paper to all members of the group.
2 Divide the group into pairs. So far as possible the members of each pair should not be known to each other.
3 Ask each pair to decide who is A and who is B.
4 Inform them all that A has about 4 minutes to interview B about their life and interests. Ideas for questions might include other members of the family, holidays, hobbies, favourite TV programmes, pet hates, favourite music. A may take notes.

   (Some groups require more prompting than others and some benefit from the use of a pre-planned form. The disadvantage of using set questions is that the responses tend to be less varied and stage 6 is less interesting to the group as a whole.)
5 Once the As have finished interviewing tell them to swap roles with B asking A questions. B may take notes. Give them the same time as you gave the As.
6 Inform them that everyone will have to make a 2 minute speech introducing their partner to the group. With some groups it is helpful if the leader has participated and leads the way. The leader can help and prompt those group members who find this task difficult.
7 After everyone has had a go it is possible to release the nervousness that the public speaking may have provoked by discussing how people felt about the exercise and allowing some sympathetic laughter.

Variations
1 The discussion at the end can be widened to include people's expectations of the course and what they hope to achieve.
2 If the game is being used to introduce a course on being interviewed for a job, the interviewee can be asked to say what they have to offer an employer. The interviewer encourages them to sell themselves.
3 This game can be used to encourage active listening by not allowing note taking.

MIME AN INTEREST

Materials: None.

Time: About 4 minutes per person.

Procedure

1 Form the group into a circle or at least so that they can all see each other.
2 Ask them to think of an interest that they can mime, e.g. an athletics enthusiast might run on the spot, a musician might mime playing an instrument.
3 Without any further talking each person in turn, including the leader, is to mime their interest and the rest of the group are to try to remember that person's mime.
4 Explain to the group that they are now nearly ready to start the game but there will be a few minutes' practice before the game starts. The procedure is a person claps their hands, performs their own mime, claps their hands again and points at someone else and **without hesitation** performs their mime.

Sequence of actions

CLAP → MIME *OWN* → CLAP → POINT TO → MIME *THEIR*
HANDS   MIME   HANDS   SOMEONE   MIME

(Be prepared to repeat this procedure a few times before everyone has the idea.)

The game proceeds by the person who was pointed out repeating this process without hesitation and so on.
5 After a few minutes' practice the game can change into a knockout with people being eliminated if they hesitate before performing the other person's mime or if they mime the wrong one.

Variations

If the purpose of the game is to warm the group up, then miming Indian names, e.g. Sitting Bull, Running Water, Little Owl, can be fun, but the element of allowing people to say something about themselves is lost.

DETECTIVE

Materials: Pens and paper.

Time: 25 minutes.

Procedure
1 Divide into pairs of people who don't know each other.
2 Distribute pens and paper to everyone.
3 Without speaking, each person should draw six items which they have used in the last three months. They should choose items which will help the other person to discover something about themselves and their interests, e.g. a person interested in climbing might draw strong boots or a rope; a musician might draw an instrument or a musical note. It does not matter if some of the drawings are not very good as this adds to the general fun and gives the Detective more to do.
4 Give each person a turn at being the Detective and guessing as much as they can about their partner. The partner should remain silent until the Detective has finished.
5 Bring the whole group together and get each person to introduce their partner to the whole group by saying what they have managed to discover about them.

Variations
1 Instead of drawing objects each person could produce six items they have with them, e.g. keys, pens, membership cards. The Detective examines these and the way the person is dressed to guess something about them. This works best in a group with a variety of backgrounds.
2 In small groups instead of dividing into pairs, the drawings or objects can be shown to the whole group who join in the guessing.

TRUTH AND DECEPTION

Materials: Copies of personal instructions on pages 50–1.

Time: About 3–4 minutes for each group member.

Procedure

1 Distribute to each group member a copy of their instructions and remind them not to let their neighbours see them.
2 Inform the group that some people will not be telling the truth. They are not to reveal their suspicions until you invite them to do so.
3 After each person has spoken for 2 minutes invite the group to ask them questions.
4 Once everyone has spoken and been questioned start the discussion on who was telling the truth and the reasons for this impression.
5 Ask the people who deceived the group to introduce themselves to the group truthfully.

Variations

More emphasis can be placed on questioning skills during procedure 3 and on considering non-verbal communication during procedure 4.

Signs of lying vary but include someone being unable to look you in the eye, blushing, signs of anxiety such as sudden sweating, throbbing veins, nervous tics, a sudden increase in the size of the eye pupil. Jade dealers often wore dark glasses to avoid revealing what they really thought of a piece of jade brought in for them to buy.

A4 TRUTH AND DECEPTION – PERSONAL INSTRUCTIONS A

In order for group members to get to know each other you will be asked to talk about yourself for 2 minutes.

You should always tell the truth.

You might like to talk about your life history, your family and your interests.

After you have spoken you may be asked questions by the group. Answer these as honestly as possible.

Only some members of the group will be telling the truth and others will be lying. Try to spot them. Do not point them out until you are asked to by the leader.

If you know someone well who is in the group then try to let other members of the group speak about them first.

CONFIDENTIAL – *Do not let anyone see this*

A4 TRUTH AND DECEPTION – PERSONAL INSTRUCTIONS B

In order for group members to get to know each other you will be asked to talk about yourself for 2 minutes.

You should not tell the truth.

You might like to invent your life history, your family and your interests.

After you have spoken you may be asked questions by the group.

Only some members of the group will be telling the truth and others will be lying. Try to spot them. Do not point them out until you are asked to by the leader.

If you know someone well who is in the group then try to let other members of the group speak about them first.

WHAT'S MY LINE?

Materials: None.

Time: 2–3 minutes for each member.

Procedure

1 Position the group so that someone doing a mime can be seen by all the other group members.
2 Ask them all to think of something they do regularly and how they could make a short mime of it or mime only a small part of the action.
3 After the mime the group guesses what is being done. To help in this process they may ask up to twelve questions to which the person doing the mime can answer only 'Yes' or 'No'.

Variations

Use a time limit for questioning rather than counting the number of questions.

Self-awareness

Aims

1 To provide opportunities for self-exploration in an emotionally safe environment.
2 To increase awareness of some of the ways we form views of ourselves and the ways these views can change.

General comments

B1 **Auction of pet hates**, B2 **Truth game** and B3 **Goldfish bowl discussion** all provide opportunities for group members to compare aspects of their own behaviour and feelings with other members of the group.

B5 **Group values** not only encourages the exploration of personal values but also explores how personal values relate to participation in the group.

B6 **Labels** looks at the possibility of improving a person's self-image.

GAME	TIME	GROUP	MATERIALS
B1 PET HATES AUCTION	40 minutes	More than 5	Blackboard/flipchart Token money useful but not essential
B2 TRUTH GAME	30 minutes minimum	Any size	Prepared Cards
B3 GOLDFISH BOWL DISCUSSION	About 40 minutes	8 or more	None
B4 ROLE SWAP	About 40 minutes	To work in pairs	None
B5 GROUP VALUES	1-1½ hours	10 or more	Pens & copies of the quiz
B6 LABELS	1 hour	Any size	Copies of quiz

Other suitable games: G4, K3, K4.

AUCTION OF PET HATES

Materials

Blackboard/flipchart to write up suggestions of the group (see page 55).
Two pages of mock money for each participant (see pages 56–7).

Time: 40 minutes.

Procedure

1 Ask the group to shout out their pet hates and the things they most like to moan about. It is important that these are written up without comment even if some seem silly. They may prove useful later. The list must have more suggestions than the number of members of the group. There is no upper limit to the size of the list.

2 Introduce the idea of token money. This is most easily done by giving £100 of mock money to each person. Some groups can use matches or are willing to keep their own record of money spent.

3 Tell the group that you are now going to auction the list of pet hates. They are to try to buy as many of their hates as possible or they may choose to spend most of their money on the thing they hate most. Only one of each item will be sold and that will be to the highest bidder.

4 Proceed to the auction. This should be as realistic as possible. Open the bidding with:

Who will give me £40 for this pet hate? Well, £30 then. £20?

It speeds things up if you take only bids of £5 or more in the early stages of the bidding. When everyone has finished bidding it can be closed by the traditional:

Going for the first time . . . Going for the second time . . . Gone!

The item is then considered sold to the highest bidder and that person's name can be written on the blackboard/flipchart next to the purchased item.

Don't worry if no one bids for an item, just pass on to the next one.

5 Once the auction is finished ask each person to say why they bought particular hates and encourage others to join in or to put the other side, especially if prejudices are involved.

Variations

1 List and auction the group's pet loves.
2 Get more vocal members of the group to take turns at being the auctioneer, with shyer members taking in the money and writing up the names of the highest bidders.

B1 AUCTION OF PET HATES

Sample list from a group of seven young adults:

Crossroads	* Managers	Vandals
Cruelty to kids	Wasps	Police
Waste	Next door's cat	Untidiness
Local football club	Marriage	Old cars
Nagging women	Conceited people	Rapists
Winter	Rats	Slow drivers
Hypocrisy	Prejudice	* Fox hunting
Income tax	Do-gooders	Terrorists
* Women drivers		

* These items formed the basis of a lively discussion with several points of view being put forward.

TRUTH GAME

Materials: Prepared cards. Ideas for questions are on page 59.

Time: 30 minutes or more depending on group size.

Procedure

1 Place the cards face down in the middle of the group.
2 Explain to the group:

> *Each card has a question on the other side. At each person's turn he/she will take a card and try to answer the question as truthfully as possible. Anyone who feels unable to answer says 'Pass' and gives the card to the next person.*

NB. This game works best if the leader is willing to take a turn and to answer honestly. It is also important that the type of questions are appropriate to the group and are not more embarrassing or revealing than the group can bear.

3 Some of the answers will provoke discussion and depending on the time available this can be encouraged.

Variations

If there are shy members in the group it may help to draw them into the game by getting them to shuffle the cards before the game starts and to hand a card to a person at the start of each turn.

SAMPLE QUESTIONS

— What do you do best?

— What sort of TV programmes do you like?

— If you won £1000 what would you spend it on?

— What makes you laugh the most?

— Who do you like most in the group?

— What was your happiest moment?

— If you were someone else who would you want to be?

— What has pleased you most today?

— What will you be doing in ten years' time?

— What lie have you told recently?

— What scares you the most?

— What embarrasses you?

— When was the last time you cried?

— What angered you most in the last week?

— Who would you most like to spend an evening with?

GOLDFISH BOWL DISCUSSION

Materials: None.

Time: Usually about 40 minutes but can be varied according to the needs of the group.

Procedure

1 Divide the group into half, either at random or by sex according to the subject and the objectives of the discussion. They should be arranged so that one half forms an inner circle where they can talk easily to each other. The other half should position themselves outside this circle in such a way that they can hear and see what happens in the inner circle. This outer group will remain silent during the discussion and act as observers. They must not interfere with the discussion.

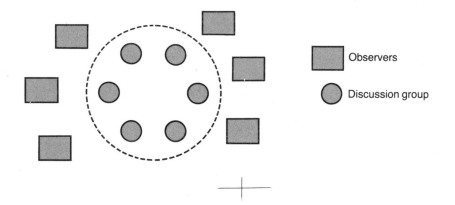

Observers

Discussion group

2 Encourage the discussion group to discuss a chosen topic as freely as possible. In a mixed-sex group obvious topics are the female view of males and vice versa. Other successful topics include the police, race relations, experiments on animals. Generally any topic which interests the group or excites strong prejudices works well. You may wish to impose a time limit on the discussion. It is often necessary to stop the observers becoming involved in the discussion.

3 After the discussion ask the observers what they saw happening in the discussion. The idea of this is not to have a repeat of the original discussion but to look at examples of prejudice, who listened or responded most to the discussion, who obstructed the discussion and what effect the discussion had on the observers.

4 Repeat the process with the observers and the discussion group swapping positions and roles.

Variations

1 This exercise can be combined with G3 **The mace**. One of the observers can be asked to plot the route of the Mace.

ROLE SWAP

Materials: None.

Time: About 40 minutes. The time can be varied according to the needs of the group.

Procedure

1 Divide the group into pairs.
2 Ask each pair to decide who is A and who is B.
3 B will act out how A would behave in a selected situation. To prepare for this they have 10 minutes to discuss how A would behave in the situation that has been selected by them or by the leader.
4 The possible situations are endless but the following have worked well.

The latecomer	How someone enters a class or meeting late.
The interview	How someone sits and talks when they are being interviewed.
The travel agent's	How someone behaves when making a difficult decision about where to go on holiday.
Breaking bad news	How someone would tell someone bad news.
A lovers' tiff	How someone behaves during an argument with someone they are fond of.
Helping a friend	How someone would help a friend in difficulty or trouble.

5 B receives continual guidance from A who has the benefit of seeing his/her own behaviour from the outside.
6 Repeat with A acting out B's behaviour.
7 Give the partners time to discuss the experience afterwards.

Variations

The role play may involve others who play the interviewer, the friend in trouble, etc.

GROUP VALUES

Materials: Pens and copies of the quiz on pages 64–5.

Time: 1 hour to 1½ hours.

Procedure

1 Distribute the quiz about personal values. Ask each person to fill the quiz in. They are not to discuss it and are to keep their answers to themselves at this stage. You may need to go through the instructions but avoid commenting on the list or revealing your own preferences.

2 After everyone has completed the quiz each member of the group is to write down a list of the people present. The names are to be ranked according to each person's participation in the group. The person who participates most will be first and the least participating person will be last with the others ranked in order between them.

3 Everyone reads out their list and the individual group members record their position in each list.

4 Divide the group into sub-groups of 4 or 5 people. Each sub-group has members who have been ranked as having similar participation levels, e.g. a sub-group of those who participate most and sub-group(s) of those in the middle of the range.

5 Each sub-group is to decide which three values it thinks are best. So far as possible the decisions are to be unanimous. They must make a decision by the end of the time limit of 20 minutes.

6 After the discussion give them 5 minutes for each sub-group to elect a spokesperson and to prepare a brief report of what has happened.

7 Bring the larger group together and ask one person from each sub-group to report their findings. This will stimulate further discussion which can be focussed on:

- *has the exercise helped you to decide what your values are or to reconsider any of them?*
- *was making a group decision about the values more or less difficult?*
- *did different groups make different decisions?*
- *how do you propose to put your values into action? Will this involve experimenting with new behaviour?*

It may help to distribute a prepared list of group members' names or to distribute name tags if the group does not know each other.

B5 GROUP VALUES – QUIZ

Read through the list and select four statements which you think describe the most valuable characteristics.

Write the numbers 1–4 next to them starting with the most valuable and putting 4 next to the least valuable of the four.

It is valuable to be:

able to react quickly without thinking ☐

careful ☐

competing with others ☐

critical ☐

different from everyone else ☐

doing one's best ☐

doing lots of different things ☐

friendly ☐

funny ☐

getting a lot done ☐

getting on in the world ☐

having a good time ☐

honest ☐

independent ☐

keen to try new experiences ☐

kind to others ☐

loyal ☐

making things ☐

powerful ☐

reliable ☐

rich ☐

right ☐

seen with the right people ☐

sure ☐

taking risks ☐

tolerant ☐

On the back of this sheet write down the names of all those doing this quiz. Next to their names place a number starting with 1 for the person who has participated most and ending with the highest number for the person who has participated least.

LABELS

Materials: Copies of the quiz, on pages 68–9, and pens.

Time: 1 hour.

Procedure

1 Distribute the quiz. Go through the instructions with the group.
2 Stress they need not reveal their answers to anyone else if they do not want to. Give them up to 10 minutes to complete the quiz. Not everyone will feel able to write down twelve labels about themselves as different people have different numbers of labels. A few have only labels they like or don't like about themselves. They should not be pressurized into pretending to have extra labels. It is also important to avoid making favourable or critical remarks about particular labels.
3 Once the quiz has been completed divide the group into pairs or threes and ask them to talk about what they have written. Remind them that they can keep some things to themselves if they want to. Topics for discussion include:

   ● do you share any labels with other people in your group?
   ● where do you think your labels have come from?

Give them 10 minutes for the discussion.
4 Bring the whole group together and go through the topics for discussion comparing different groups' findings.
5 During the discussion you may wish to make the following points:

Labels come from a variety of sources.
   ● Those which are identified as 'I've always been like this' probably come from the early years of life. Relatives often repeat saying things to very young children about their looks, personality or behaviour. Others may come from more recent experiences especially the comments of friends and people with power over us. We may take on these labels because we are too small, too busy or too powerless to reject them. **However, it is possible to reconsider these labels and to change them if you want to. You are not stuck with them.**

Advantages of labels
- *They make life seem more simple and straightforward. By counting up the labels we like about ourselves and comparing them with those we dislike about ourselves we get a sense of personal worth, e.g. I am basically good/nice OR I am not a worthwhile person.*
- *They make us feel secure and comfortable because we feel we know what we are like.*
- *They give us a guide about how we should behave as we can try to live up to our labels, e.g. 'I am good'/'I am bad'/'I am always taking risks.' They can give us permission to do things, e.g. if my label is 'I am weak willed' I am more likely to eat that extra cream bun. They can also give excuses to avoid doing things because 'I am not like that.'*

Labels can be dangerous
- *They can mislead us into thinking that they are permanent and fixed. They are not like a hole in the heart or an infected appendix which require operations to change them. Labels can be changed if we choose to.*
- *They can keep us in fixed patterns of behaviour, e.g. 'I am unemotional' may mean we do not cry in a tragedy or express our anger when it is justified and it might be better to reveal our feelings.*
- *Labels can be an excuse and allow us to opt out of things we might otherwise do. We can avoid new experiences by saying 'I am not like that' because proposed experience does not fit our labels.*

6 The final stage of the exercise is intended to assist with changing unwanted labels.

Ask the group to return to their previous pairs or threes. They are to choose a label which they do not like about themselves *and* they are willing to talk about.

7 They are to discuss:

- under what circumstances do I behave as described by the label, e.g. where? when? with whom? how often? Describe a typical situation.
- what do I actually do or not do which earns the label?
- if I want to change any of the labels what could I do to make the label inappropriate?

8 The leader can go round the small groups, encourage all attempts at changes and foster a helpful and caring atmosphere.

B6 LABELS – QUIZ

Complete the statements beginning 'I am . . .' under the two headings below. The first list describes things you like about yourself and the second list things you do not like. Examples of things other people have written include: 'I am a happy-go-lucky person', 'I am friendly' and 'I am a trouble-maker.'

Try to put six in both lists. Some people find they can think of only three or four things. Most people can think of several things for each list. There are no right or wrong answers.

Things I like about myself

I am ....

I am ....

I am ....

I am ....

I am ....

I am ....

Things I don't like about myself

I am ....

I am ....

I am ....

I am ....

I am ....

I am ....

After you have divided into small groups select the labels you are willing to talk about. You do not have to reveal anything you do not want to.

In the first discussion you will be asked to consider:

- do you share any labels with other people in your group?
- at what stage in your life do you think these labels were first applied to you?

In the second discussion you may find it helpful to concentrate on the labels you would most like to change. You will be asked to talk about:

- under what circumstances do I behave as described by the label, e.g. where? when? with whom? how often? Describe a typical situation.
- what do I actually do or not do which earns the label?
- if I want to change any of the labels what could I do to make the label inappropriate?

C.

Social skills

Aims

1 To explore the type of social skill appropriate to particular situations.
2 To create a supportive environment where people can learn to improve their social skills from others.
3 To help people towards planning how to improve their social skills.

General comments

Social skills like other types of skill require both a knowledge of what to do as well as an ability to perform that skill. Both the knowledge and the ability can be refined or improved with practice. This process need not stop at a particular point in life. With only slight changes all the exercises in this section have been used with a wide age range from young teenagers to adults.

C1 **Predicaments** allows a group of people to explore how others would react in tricky situations as well as the social skills involved.

C2 **Role play** provides general hints on how to set one up. This can be an invaluable method of exploring all kinds of situations in a relatively safe way which allows people to experiment with their social skills.

C3 **The job interview** is an example of one way of setting up a role play as a means of exploring and improving the skills involved. In a period of high unemployment these skills can be essential.

C4 **Social skills with others** is a quiz to help identify the skills someone wishes to improve as the start of the process of doing something about it.

GAME / QUIZ	TIME	GROUP	MATERIALS
C1 PREDICAMENTS	20 minutes - 1 hour	5-10 per group	Prepared cards
C2 ROLE PLAY	Varies	Any size	Prepared instructions
C3 THE JOB INTERVIEW	45 minutes - 1 hour	4 per group	Pens and paper Copies of instructions
C4 MY FIVE BEST POINTS	30 - 45 minutes	5-8 per group	Pens and paper
C5 SOCIAL SKILLS WITH OTHERS	45 minutes	Any size	Pens Copies of quiz

Other suitable games: H5, I5, I6.

PREDICAMENTS

Materials: Prepared cards (see examples on page 73). There should be more cards than the number of people in the group.

Time: 20 minutes to 1 hour.

Procedure

1 Place the pile of prepared cards in the centre of the group.
2 Explain that each person in turn will take a card from the pile. They will read out what is written on the card and then say what they would do in the situation described on the card. If someone does not want to answer a particular card they may say 'Pass' and take the next card. The rejected card is placed in the unused pile.
3 The first person takes a card and reads out the predicament, e.g. 'Your house is on fire. You have time to save two things.' The group can then make comments and a discussion may follow. Keep reminding the group there may be more than one correct answer. Encourage them to explore the social skills involved.
4 Continue the process until everyone has had one or more goes.

Variations

1 Sound recordings of the first response to the predicament can be used to help the discussion.
2 The examples suggested for the cards can be changed. It is important that the predicaments are relevant to the group. Some groups can suggest their own predicaments before the game begins. This can be done by distributing blank cards and asking them to write predicaments on them. They can be collected in and shuffled and then used in the usual way.

EXAMPLES

What would you do if . . . ?

- You are accused of stealing some money by someone in authority, e.g. headmaster, police officer. You did not do it but you know who did.
- A friend asks you for advice. She, his girlfriend, is unexpectedly pregnant.
- You lend £10 to a friend. Repayment was promised for last Wednesday. Your friend seems to be avoiding you and has not paid any money.
- A friend offers you a stolen video recorder at a very low price.
- Someone seems to be following you late one night. There is no one else around.
- Your house is on fire. You have time to save two things.
- Your best friend admits to being homosexual or lesbian.
- You are swimming naked in a river when a family settles down to have a picnic near your clothes. The water is cold and you would like to get out.
- You see a man you don't know looking into a neighbour's windows at the back of their house.
- Someone is spreading lies about you.
- Someone keeps picking on your best friend.
- You see two young men beating up a policeman.
- You find a tramp lying on a busy pavement. He could be ill or drunk. Other people are stepping over him.

ROLE PLAY – GENERAL INSTRUCTIONS

Materials: Paper and pens to allow group members to take notes. Props can be useful to help create the setting. If the real thing is not available it is possible to improvise, e.g. a table can represent a shop counter or if it is laid on its side it can become a prisoner's dock in a court room.

Time: Variable. The more you ask the participants to prepare for their role the longer the time needed.

PROCEDURE

1 Identify a situation which you want the group to become skilled in.

2 Prepare written instructions for those taking part. Written instructions reassure the more nervous participants and give them something to refer to if they become uncertain.

    The instructions should be short, clear and written in general terms so that the person playing the role can bring their own experience and skills to the role. They should include enough background information to keep the situation realistic. You may wish to use observers as they can add to the value of discussions after the role play. They become much more involved if they also receive instructions about what they are expected to comment on. C3 **The job interview** provides examples of instruction sheets.

3 Distribute the instructions and allow time for questions and answers. The aim is to ensure that everyone knows what is expected of them and to avoid all interruptions to the flow of the role play once it is started.

4 Ask the group(s) how they wish to use the space they have and how they intend to use any props that they have. This can help the role players towards finding their roles so that they play them with conviction. It is also an opportunity to provide information which keeps the exercise realistic, e.g. the way things are usually arranged in this particular situation.

5 Start the role play. Even the most carefully planned role play will sometimes take on a life of its own and take unexpected turns. Unless this threatens the whole purpose of the exercise it is best to note how it happened and to discuss it later rather than interrupt the activity.

6 After the role play nearly as much time again can be usefully spent

7 4

debriefing the participants and observers (if any). Often some of the participants are excited or emotionally aroused by the experience and they will want a few minutes to discuss with each other what they had expected other role players to do and incidents within the role play. Allowing them to do this helps to reduce any tensions and assists the players to return to their everyday roles.

7 The more formal discussion of the experience may be started by asking them:

- *How did you enjoy the experience?*
- *How did you like playing your role?*

The transition from discussing their feelings to the skills they needed to use in the role play can be made by:

- *What did you find difficult?*
- *What skills did you use?*
- *What worked well and what skills helped it to work well?*

It is helpful to concentrate on the ways certain skills have helped certain people along and eased difficult situations as this will encourage others to learn them.

For criticism to lead to changes in behaviour it is most useful if it is phrased positively and is specific. 'It would be better if you talked more loudly' gives someone the hope of being both better heard as well as better regarded if they make a change. They also know exactly what is expected of them. Saying much the same thing negatively, 'It would be better if you did not talk so quietly', can leave a person concentrating on their sense of failure rather than striving to improve.

Negative unspecific criticism is to be discouraged. If someone states, 'You are useless', the recipient is both uncertain of the changes needed to improve things as well as emotionally concentrating on failure rather than on the possibility of success. If this happens it helps to get the person making the criticism to restate it in a sentence starting with, 'It would be better if you . . .' This will also help the recipient of the criticism.

The final stage of the discussion should focus on:

- *What have you learned from the experience?*
- *What skills do you need to develop or improve?*
- *What is the next step in improving them?*

It is good practice to ensure that each participant has an idea of what they are going to do next to improve their skills.

Variations

1 Spoken briefs can be used with more experienced groups as they are less likely to need the emotional support of a written brief.

2 In some situations the participants may be able to write their own briefs, e.g. if a magistrates' court is being role played the court officials might be given prepared briefs but the defendant and witnesses might be encouraged to write their own.

THE JOB INTERVIEW
An Example of a Role Play

Materials: Pens and paper. Copies of the instruction sheets on pages 78–83.

Time: 45 minutes to 1 hour.

Procedure

1 Divide the group into fours and ask them to decide who will be the interviewer and who the applicant. The other two are observers.
2 Distribute the writing materials and instruction sheets and answer any questions about the role play.
3 Ask the applicant to tell one of the observers the kind of job they wish to apply for and to describe the kind of work involved. The choice should be the kind of job they would apply for if they saw it advertised tomorrow. The observer is to give this information to the interviewer. The interviewer and applicant must not speak to each other during the preparation stage.
4 Give them 10 minutes' preparation time. One observer is to assist the applicant and the other the interviewer.
5 The fours are to arrange themselves for the interview. The observers should be to one side to avoid interfering but should be close enough to hear.
6 Allow about 15 minutes for the interview.
7 After the interview ask the observers to tell the others their answers to the questions on their instruction sheets. The interviewer and applicant should also give the answers to the questions at the end of their instructions.

Variations

1 Repeat the role play until everyone has played each part.
2 You may wish to end by bringing the large group together to brainstorm the skills which helped the applicants to help themselves. With these written on a blackboard or flipchart, have a general discussion along the lines suggested in C2 **Role play** procedure 7.
3 I5 **The job interview (variation)** also looks at the skills involved in asking questions.

C3 THE JOB INTERVIEW – INTERVIEWER INSTRUCTION SHEET

Before beginning the interview the applicant will tell one of the observers the type of job he/she is applying for and will give a brief description of the kind of work that is involved. This information will be passed on to you.

You will then have 10 minutes to prepare your questions as though you were interviewing the applicant for the job. *You must not talk to the applicant during this preparation stage.* You may obtain help by discussing it with an observer.

Interviewers are often concerned to know:

- Why are you interested in this particular job?
- What do you know about the job?
- What experience or skills do you have which make(s) you suitable for the job?
- What other interests do you have?

They may also wish to know about attitudes to timekeeping, smartness or to any of the obvious difficulties of a particular job, e.g. being away from home for long periods, facing up to danger or other unpleasant experiences.

You should plan your questions to draw as much information from the applicant as possible.

When the interview starts you are to treat it as though you are an employer considering whether to offer the applicant a job.

After the interview be ready to answer:

What did the applicant do or say which would encourage me to offer him/her the job?

C3 THE JOB INTERVIEW – APPLICANT INSTRUCTION SHEET

One of the observers will ask you to name the type of job you would like to apply for. You will be asked to give the job title, e.g. nurse, shop assistant, bricklayer, computer operator, and to give a brief description of the type of work that is involved. It will be helpful if you try to make your choice as realistic as possible.

When you have given this information to the observer you have 10 minutes to think about your answers to the types of questions you might get in a job interview. *You must not talk to the interviewer at this stage.* You may obtain help by discussing it with an observer.

Applicants are often asked:

- Why are you interested in this particular job?
- What do you know about the job?
- What experience or skills do you have which make(s) you suitable for the job?
- What other interests do you have?

They may also wish to know about your attitudes to timekeeping, smartness or to any of the obvious difficulties of a particular job, e.g. being away from home for long periods, facing up to danger or other unpleasant experiences.

When the interview starts you are to treat it as though you are an applicant for the job.

After the interview be ready to answer:

What did I think went well and would help to get me the job? What would I like to do better?

C3 THE JOB INTERVIEW – OBSERVER INSTRUCTION SHEET

a. Preparation stage

Ask the person playing the applicant:

- *what kind of job do you want to apply for?*
- *what do you expect to do in that kind of job?*

Encourage the applicant to be as realistic as possible. It should be the sort of job they would apply for if they saw a vacancy advertised. If the answer is a long one you may wish to take notes.

Pass the information on to the person playing the interviewer. *The applicant and interviewer should not talk to each other at this stage.* They will be given 10 minutes to prepare for their interview. One of the observers should help the interviewer and the other the applicant.

b. The interview

During the interview you should sit quietly to one side where you can hear what is being said. Do not interrupt them.

You are to observe what happens. You make take notes. Afterwards you should be prepared to comment on:

1 Did all those taking part speak clearly so that they could hear each other?
2 Is there anything anyone can do to improve the way they are heard, e.g. speak more slowly or louder?
3 Which of the interviewer's questions seemed most likely to be used in a real interview?
4 Which questions encouraged the applicant to speak most?
5 What did the applicant say which seemed to improve the chance of being employed?
6 How did the applicant and interviewer sit during the interview? Did the posture he/she took suggest they were interested or bored? (Be prepared to imitate their postures when you explain your answer.)

MY FIVE BEST POINTS

Materials: Pens and paper.

Time: 30–45 minutes.

Procedure

1 Ask the participants to divide themselves into groups of between five and eight.
2 Inform them:

I would like you to think what your five best points are for a few minutes. They may be your attitudes, feelings or something you can do. At the same time I would like you to think of situations where you have demonstrated these best points. You can make notes about these if you wish to.

When you are ready I will ask everyone to take a turn at describing their five best points to their group and to give brief examples. While you are speaking, the other members of your group will listen to you without making any comments.

3 Run the game. Be prepared for some of the participants to be hesitant or embarrassed at the beginning. This passes as they begin to enjoy thinking of themselves positively. It is a particularly useful game for boosting the self-image of people who usually think of themselves in terms of their bad points. It also serves many other purposes because at the same time they are practising self-evaluation, public speaking and other skills.

4 When everyone has had a turn ask them to discuss:
   - what did you feel about the game?
   - do we need to be shy about revealing our good points?

This will help them to explore any aspects of the game which felt strange and to look for opportunities to present themselves in a positive way to others.

SOCIAL SKILLS WITH OTHERS

Materials: Copies of the quiz (on pages 86–7) for all members.

Time: 45 minutes.

Procedure

1 Distribute the quiz and go through the instructions at the top of the quiz with the group.
2 Explain that they will not be required to show their answers to anyone they don't want to. The answers are for their own benefit. The more truthful they are the more helpful they will find it.
3 Give the group 10–15 minutes to complete the quiz.
4 Divide the group into threes or fours. Ask them to see if they can agree on which skills they most wish to improve. They do not need to show their answers to the others unless they want to. Allow them 10 minutes for the discussion.
5 Ask each group to report back to you. You may wish to use this information to plan further work. It is good practice to try to ensure that they all know what they are going to do next to improve at least one skill. This may range from attending a course or evening class to observing a friend who already possesses that skill.

C5 SOCIAL SKILLS WITH OTHERS – QUIZ

There are no right or wrong answers in this quiz. The more truthful you are the more helpful it will be. You will not be asked to show your answers to anyone unless you are willing to do so.

Read through the list of some of the skills we use when we try to get on with other people. Place a tick in the box which describes how good or bad you are at that skill, e.g. if you feel you are neither good nor bad at starting talking to someone you know, your answer would be:

Starting talking to someone you know [Very bad] [Bad] [Average] [Good] [Very good]

1 Starting talking to someone you know [Very bad] [Bad] [Average] [Good] [Very good]

2 Starting talking to someone you do not know [Very bad] [Bad] [Average] [Good] [Very good]

3 Keeping a conversation going [Very bad] [Bad] [Average] [Good] [Very good]

4 Asking someone to explain something you have not understood [Very bad] [Bad] [Average] [Good] [Very good]

5 Listening to what others say [Very bad] [Bad] [Average] [Good] [Very good]

6 Saying what you feel [Very bad] [Bad] [Average] [Good] [Very good]

7 Standing up for what you believe in [Very bad] [Bad] [Average] [Good] [Very good]

8 Saying sorry [Very bad] [Bad] [Average] [Good] [Very good]

9 Asking for information, e.g. What time is the next bus? [Very bad] [Bad] [Average] [Good] [Very good]

10 Asking for someone to leave you alone	[Very bad]	[Bad]	[Average]	[Good] [Very good]
11 Saying thank you	[Very bad]	[Bad]	[Average]	[Good] [Very good]
12 Speaking in front of a group	[Very bad]	[Bad]	[Average]	[Good] [Very good]
13 Speaking to someone of the same sex	[Very bad]	[Bad]	[Average]	[Good] [Very good]
14 Speaking to someone of the opposite sex	[Very bad]	[Bad]	[Average]	[Good] [Very good]
15 Making a complaint	[Very bad]	[Bad]	[Average]	[Good] [Very good]
16 Keeping your temper	[Very bad]	[Bad]	[Average]	[Good] [Very good]
17 Speaking on the telephone	[Very bad]	[Bad]	[Average]	[Good] [Very good]
18 Speaking to older people	[Very bad]	[Bad]	[Average]	[Good] [Very good]
19 Speaking to younger people	[Very bad]	[Bad]	[Average]	[Good] [Very good]
20 Knowing when to call people by their first name or Mr/Mrs . . .	[Very bad]	[Bad]	[Average]	[Good] [Very good]

When you have put a tick on every line read through the list again. Select *three* skills you would especially like to improve and underline them. E.g.

Starting to talk to someone you don't know   [Very bad] [Bad] [Average] [Good] [Very good]

You will be given the opportunity to discuss these in small groups. It will be helpful if you can think of actual circumstances when you would like to be better at your chosen skills, e.g. starting to talk to someone of an opposing sports team.

Needs awareness

Aims

1 To assist in discovering needs and then ranking them in order of importance.

2 To begin planning for satisfying those needs.

General comments

A person without needs is dead. Needs give us the energy and the drive to do things. It is possible to help people to satisfy these needs. An illustration of this process can be found at the end of D2 **Dream**. This could be used in any of the exercises in this section.

D1 **Moments in life** uses a graph or pictures as a means of easing the process of looking at needs. D2 **Dream** uses day-dreams as a starting point.

D3 **Needs discovery quiz** provides a more detailed and pre-planned approach to the same process. Both of the other two games have been used successfully as a preparation for this quiz.

The objective of all these exercises is not only to help people to identify unsatisfied needs but also to assist in planning to meet those needs. The leader and other group members can be invaluable in assisting this process.

GAME/QUIZ	TIME	GROUP	MATERIALS
D1 MOMENTS IN LIFE	30 minutes	Any size	Pens and copies of the quiz
D2 DREAM	30 minutes	Any size	Pens and paper Blackboard/ flipchart
D3 NEEDS DISCOVERY QUIZ	30 minutes	Any size	Pens and copies of quiz

MOMENTS IN LIFE

Materials: Pens and copies of the quiz on pages 90–1.

Time: 30 minutes.

Procedure

1 Ask the group to draw a graph representing their feelings about their life so far. E.g.

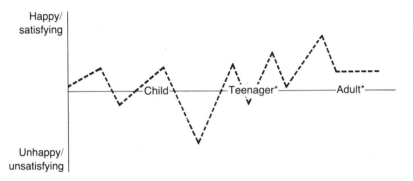

2 Divide them into small groups or pairs and ask them to explain their personal version of the graph to the others as far as they are willing to. They are not required to reveal things they do not wish to.

3 Still in the small groups ask them to say:

- *what needs do you feel have been satisfied in the past?*
- *what are the most important needs you still wish to satisfy?*
- *what can you do to go some way to satisfying those needs?*

This last stage is important and the aim is to encourage everyone to have an idea of what they could do next towards satisfying a need.

Variations

Instead of drawing a graph they could be asked to draw pictures of life three years ago and life three years in the future. These need not be good artwork but form the basis of a discussion of the same three questions. The graph/pictures are a device to ease the difficulty of starting a potentially useful discussion of needs.

D1 MOMENTS IN LIFE – QUIZ

Most people have times in their life which are more or less satisfying than others. Draw a line on the graph representing your feelings about your life so far. It does not have to be to scale so long as it means something to you.

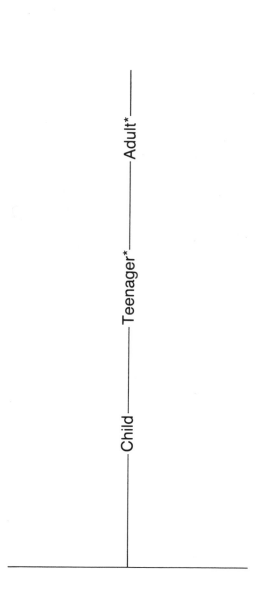

Child —————— Teenager* —————— Adult* ——————

*delete if not applicable

You will be asked to explain the graph to someone else but you are not required to talk about things if you do not want to. You can just say, 'I would sooner not speak about this at the moment but this is how I feel about it.'

After explaining the graph you will be asked to discuss:

- *what needs do you feel have been satisfied at different times in the past?*
- what are the most important needs you still wish to satisfy?
- what can you do to go some way to satisfying those needs?

You should aim to have planned at least one thing you can do to go towards satisfying that need. You may be able to help someone else do the same.

DREAM

Materials: Pens and paper for each group member. Blackboard/flipchart.

Time: 30 minutes.

Procedure

1 Tell the whole group:

> *You are to imagine a situation where there is nothing stopping you or restricting you.*
> *What would you really like to do or to be?*
> *What is your secret dream? You can keep this dream secret but think about it.*

2 Give them 2 or 3 minutes for this and ask them to write brief notes.

3 Ask them to write down five reasons why they would like to be or do what they said.

4 Ask for examples of three **reasons** (not dreams) from the group and write them up on blackboard/flipchart without comment.

5 Open it up to a general discussion. Points you might wish to make are:

   a A person without needs is dead.

   b Needs give us the drive to do things.

   c Satisfaction of needs doesn't just happen – we have to do something.

   d The things we aim at to get satisfaction can be called goals. The dream in the exercise is a goal. Identifying the reasons for the dream can help to achieve some of the dream. E.g.

Dream	To be a top football player
Reason	– physical exercise
	– enjoy appearing in public
	– thing I know most about
	– make people respect me

It may not be possible to achieve the dream, but couldn't many of the reasons be satisfied by being a referee? This could become a realistic goal if the dream is not possible for any reason.

NEEDS DISCOVERY QUIZ

Materials: Pens and a copy of the quiz on pages 94–5.

Time: 30 minutes.

Procedure

1 Distribute the quiz. Explain the instructions if this is necessary but avoid revealing how you would answer the quiz yourself.
2 After everyone has completed the quiz divide them into threes or fours. Ask them to discuss:

- *are there any needs you all share?*
- *which needs are most satisfied?*
- *which needs are least satisfied?*
- *what can you do towards satisfying your least satisfied needs?*

No one is required to reveal things they do not wish to.

D3 NEEDS DISCOVERY QUIZ

Twenty needs which many people have are listed below. The list cannot include all the possible needs so there are some blank spaces for you to write down any needs you are feeling which have been missed out.

Start by completing this column first.
Underline the needs you are feeling.

For the needs you have underlined only, put a tick in the appropriate box to say how satisfied that need is

I have a need to:

1 Relax   [Very satisfied] [Satisfied] [Not satisfied]

2 Have an exciting life   [Very satisfied] [Satisfied] [Not satisfied]

3 Be told what to do   [Very satisfied] [Satisfied] [Not satisfied]

4 Have times when things don't change   [Very satisfied] [Satisfied] [Not satisfied]

5 Have a quiet life   [Very satisfied] [Satisfied] [Not satisfied]

6 Be with people   [Very satisfied] [Satisfied] [Not satisfied]

7 Be liked by others   [Very satisfied] [Satisfied] [Not satisfied]

8 Help others   [Very satisfied] [Satisfied] [Not satisfied]

9 Be part of a team   [Very satisfied] [Satisfied] [Not satisfied]

10 Be a leader   [Very satisfied] [Satisfied] [Not satisfied]

11 Do things on my own   [Very satisfied] [Satisfied] [Not satisfied]

12	Look good	[Very satisfied]	[Satisfied]	[Not satisfied]
13	Feel physically fit	[Very satisfied]	[Satisfied]	[Not satisfied]
14	Like myself	[Very satisfied]	[Satisfied]	[Not satisfied]
15	Achieve things	[Very satisfied]	[Satisfied]	[Not satisfied]
16	Give affection	[Very satisfied]	[Satisfied]	[Not satisfied]
17	Be good at doing something	[Very satisfied]	[Satisfied]	[Not satisfied]
18	Be respected	[Very satisfied]	[Satisfied]	[Not satisfied]
19	....	[Very satisfied]	[Satisfied]	[Not satisfied]
20	....	[Very satisfied]	[Satisfied]	[Not satisfied]

When you have completed this quiz, you can divide into small groups and discuss:

- Are there any needs you all share?
- Which needs are most satisfied?
- Which needs are least satisfied?
- What can you do towards satisfying your least satisfied needs?

You need not reveal anything you do not wish to.

Goal planning

Aims

1 To encourage the view that needs can be met by realistic goal setting.
2 To provide experience of goal setting.

General comments

Nothing succeeds like success. Setting realistic goals makes success possible and when they are achieved there is satisfaction. This satisfaction will make setting off for the next goal easier.

Setting goals is made more helpful by:

● being as specific as you can be, i.e. when, where, how;
● telling your friends, as their interest may encourage you;
● setting deadlines – lots of small ones, to encourage you on your way;
● being realistic – aim to get to your nearest city not the moon.

E1 **House of cards** and E2 **Flying far** give opportunities for practising goal setting and looking at how this can improve the sense of personal satisfaction. Both finish with discussions during which the general comments about goal setting can be made.

GAME	TIME	GROUP	MATERIALS
E1 HOUSE OF CARDS	45 minutes	Capable of dividing into fives or sixes	Packs of old cards Pens and paper Blackboard/ flipchart
E2 FLYING FAR	45 minutes	Capable of dividing into pairs or threes	Paper, sellotape paperclips, Blackboard/ flipchart Large space

HOUSE OF CARDS

Materials: Old packs of cards – new cards are too smooth. Pens and paper. Blackboard or flipchart.

Time: 45 minutes.

Procedure

1 Ask each individual to estimate silently how many storeys of a card tower they can build in 5 minutes. They are to write the figure down and they must keep it to themselves.

2 Give them 5 minutes to build as tall a tower as possible. They are to write down the number of completed storeys they achieved. This figure must be kept to themselves. They will find this information useful in the next stage of the game.

3 Each individual has to publicly shout out their estimated tower height and then build as big a tower as possible in 5 minutes. The estimated figure and achieved figure are noted on a public chart or blackboard.

4 Divide the group into teams of 5 or 6. Ask the teams to estimate how many storeys they can build and have standing at the end of 5 minutes. Note their answers on a blackboard/flipchart. Up to three towers may be built side by side which allows everyone in the team to be involved. The winning team is the one with the most card house storeys standing at the end of the competition. Compare these results with their estimates.

5 Lead a discussion on:

- *did making an estimate in advance add to the sense of satisfaction or make you try harder to achieve it?*
- *did declaring your estimate publicly make any difference?*
- *did the addition of team competition make any difference?*

Variations

Other items can be used instead of cards to build a tower, e.g. building blocks, empty cans, dominoes.

FLYING FAR

Materials: Blackboard/flipchart. Paper for making paper planes. Sellotape, paperclips (large space needed indoors/outdoors).

Time: 45 minutes.

Procedure

1 Ask everyone to make paper airplanes and to test that they fly. At this stage the airplane can be made only by folding a single sheet of paper.

2 Ask them to write down how far the plane went on its longest flight. This can be measured in paces or by reference to fixed points, e.g. just past the table. These distances should be written down.

3 They are to estimate how much further they think they can make each plane fly by modifying it with more paper, sellotape, paperclips, etc. This estimate is to be written down publicly on a blackboard/flipchart. This is their goal.

4 Working in pairs or threes they are to help each other to make improvements to the plane so that it can fly further until it achieves their goal or gets as close to it as possible.

5 Organize a final flight for all the modified planes and record the distances achieved on the blackboard/flipchart.

6 Ask them to talk in their pairs/threes about:

- *what effect did setting a new goal for your plane have?*
- *did it make a difference that you told your partner(s) about this goal and that it was publicly written down?*
- *did your partner(s) help?*
- *do you now think your goal was realistic?*

7 Bring the whole group together. Go round the whole group and ask them quickly to answer the following:

- *do you think your goal was realistic?*
- *are you satisfied with the flight of the modified plane?*

This is to emphasize the link between making realistic goals which can be achieved and personal satisfaction.

You may then wish to make some of the points contained in the general comments introducing this section.

Planning what to do next

Aims

To provide an opportunity for someone who has experienced games from the previous sections to review certain aspects of their life and then make realistic goals for the future.

General comments

This quiz is intended as a personal record and not as the basis for further discussion. It could well be given to someone who has been through a sequence of games from B. **Self-awareness**, through C. **Social skills** and D. **Needs awareness** to E. **Goal planning**. It could be completed in their own time to allow them to record their considered decisions based on the experiences they have just had. Doing it in private will allow them to consider things they would not risk revealing publicly.

QUIZ	TIME	GROUP	MATERIALS
F1 PLANNING WHAT TO DO NEXT	30-40 minutes of time on one's own	Any size	Copy of quiz

PLANNING WHAT TO DO NEXT

NB. There are no right or wrong answers to any of the questions on these sheets.

You will not be asked to reveal anything to other people you wish to keep to yourself.

YOUR LIFE UP TO NOW

It can help in planning the future to look at the past so that you can build on the good experiences and try to avoid less happy ones.

Draw a line, on each of the graphs that follow, which represents your feelings about your life so far. Each of the graphs is about a different aspect of life.

You may find it helpful to write notes on the graph to explain the ups and downs of the line you have drawn. This saves worrying about drawing to scale.

E.g.

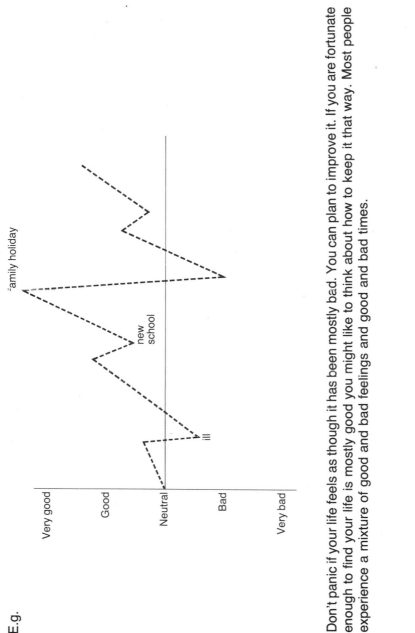

Don't panic if your life feels as though it has been mostly bad. You can plan to improve it. If you are fortunate enough to find your life is mostly good you might like to think about how to keep it that way. Most people experience a mixture of good and bad feelings and good and bad times.

HOW DO YOU FEEL ABOUT YOUR

. . . life with family and friends?

Very good

Good

Neutral

Bad

Very bad

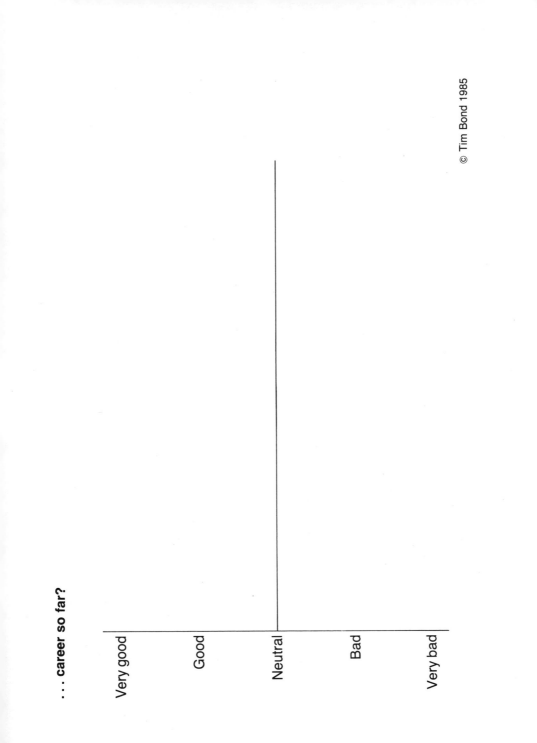

. . . career so far?

Very good

Good

Neutral

Bad

Very bad

© Tim Bond 1985

. . . personal satisfaction?

- Very good
- Good
- Neutral
- Bad
- Very bad

Look at the graphs. Thinking about the best moments in your life so far, write down up to five things you like best about yourself.

Things I like about myself

1 I am ....

2 I am ....

3 I am ....

4 I am ....

5 I am ....

Now look again at the graphs. Write down up to five things you like least about yourself.

Things I don't like about myself

1 I am ....

2 I am ....

3 I am ....

4 I am ....

5 I am ....

Again there are no right answers although most people think of themselves as a mixture of things they like and dislike. These ideas about ourselves vary throughout life and to a large extent we can get rid of the labels we don't like with planning and effort. *You are not stuck with the things you don't like about yourself. You can change them.*

Trying to change things you don't like about yourself is often made easier by thinking of a typical event which seems to illustrate the undesirable label and planning to change that event e.g.

The label I don't like

I am ..underiable..........................

Typical event

...I agree to meeting friends
and then don't go...............
....

Select a label you don't like about yourself and which you would like to change. Write down a situation which seems to show the label is true. It helps to be as detailed as possible so there are more questions to help you describe the situation.

The label I don't like	Typical event
I am	....
	....
When does it happen?	....
Where does it happen?	....
Who else is involved?	....

If this event were to be repeated it could be improved by changes in some or all of the following ways:

What practical things can be changed to improve the situation?

. . . .

. . . .

What weaknesses or failings need to be improved in myself?

. . . .

. . . .

What can I do to help myself?

. . . .

. . . .

What help do I need from others?

. . . .

. . . .

If you have left the middle two questions in the last box blank it may be worth thinking about them again. Often it is changes in yourself which are easiest to achieve because they are within your control. Even small changes can produce surprising results and a different outcome.

You are now in a position to plan some goals which you can achieve.

Look again at the answers in the last box you filled in. Then write up the goals you can achieve and state the time you intend to have achieved them by.

It is important to be as realistic as possible. Choosing something you can achieve will encourage you to try. If you do achieve your goal, you will find that nothing succeeds like success and you want to do more to improve the quality of your life.

What would I like to achieve?	When?
1	....
2	....
3	....
4	....

It is now up to you to try to put it into action.

Don't get discouraged if it takes several attempts to achieve your goals. Remember the better times in your life: the prize for succeeding is even more of these better times.

If like many people you find this kind of process helpful, you may like to use it to plan ways of improving other situations. Remember there are no right and wrong solutions. It's what helps you that matters.

During life your needs and goals will probably change. It is useful to stop and think them through every now and again. It helps to keep you in control of your own life and to gain more satisfaction from it.

G.

Deciding who is important

Aims

1 To help in ranking people's importance in a person's own life or within the group.
2 To explore the feelings of being important or unimportant within a group of people.

General comments

G1 **Guess the leader** is a fun game enjoyed particularly by younger people. It provides opportunities to start people thinking about how we become aware of powerful individuals when we walk into an established group. G2 **The wheel** provides a structured way of analysing who is important in a group member's life outside the group. G3 **The mace** focusses on what is happening within the group. Both exercises can be used with a wide variety of age groups and backgrounds. G4 **The mouse that turns** is a more difficult game to run because it draws attention to the existing power structure within a group and then unsettles it as the basis for discussion. This works with most groups but special care is needed if you suspect any of the participants of bullying; this could not only affect the game but could make life unpleasant for the quieter members of the group afterwards.

GAME	TIME	GROUP	MATERIALS
G1 GUESS THE LEADER	30 minutes	Best in groups of 6-10	None
G2 THE WHEEL	20 minutes	Any size	Pens & paper
G3 THE MACE	10 minutes or longer	Best in groups of 5-10	Ball or other object Pens & paper
G4 THE MOUSE THAT TURNS	45 minutes	Best in groups of 6-12	Pens & paper Container as a ballot box Copies of elected leader briefing sheet

GUESS THE LEADER

Materials: None.

Time: 30 minutes.

Procedure

1 One person is to move away so that they cannot see or hear what is happening in the rest of the group.
2 The group appoints one person to be their leader who will start the clapping, head-tapping, arm-swinging or any other movement. The rest of the group copy the leader.
3 The person who has been outside returns and tries to guess who is the leader, he/she is to give reasons for each choice. The leader will change the movements about every 30 seconds.
4 Repeat the process with different people outside and leading.
5 This is a very light-hearted way of introducing ideas about how we become aware of who is the powerful person in a group, e.g. we notice others waiting to see which way he or she will go, eye contact, eye level. The organizer has opportunities to emphasize these points when the person trying to spot the leader gives the reasons for a particular choice.

Variations

This can also be used as a fun introduction to non-verbal communications to sharpen observation skills.

THE WHEEL

Materials: Pens and paper.

Time: 20 minutes.

Procedure
1 Distribute pens and paper.
2 Ask everyone to think of between 6 and 10 important people in their lives.
3 Tell them:

You are to draw a wheel but the spokes are to be all different lengths. At the end of each spoke you are to write the name of one of the people you thought of. The person who means the most to you will be nearest the centre or the axle and the least important will be the furthest out. The others will be ranked according to importance in between. E.g.

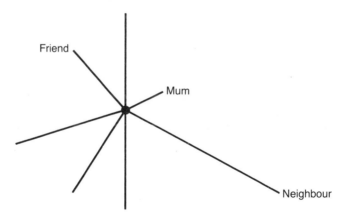

This is a device which is sometimes used in management training when it is used to look at the importance of people at work. It can also be used for our personal lives as a means of recording who is most important to us at any particular time. The position of the people on the wheel will vary over periods of time.

4 Ask them to divide into pairs or threes and to discuss:

- *how much has your chart changed in the last year?*
- *what would you like it to be like in a year's time?*
- *what can you do to help that change take place?*

THE MACE

Materials: A ball or a book or anything that can be passed around the group but is large enough to be visible to the whole group. This can be called the Mace. In the House of Commons this is the symbol of the Speaker's authority.

Time: 10 minutes or longer.

Procedure

1 Establish a topic most of the group is interested in talking about. This can be done by brainstorming (see page 26), or for suggestions see pages 55, 60).
2 Inform the group that only the person who is holding the Mace can speak. You may wish to tell them that you will be recording who gets the Mace and how often.
3 As the game proceeds you will probably have to keep reminding them of the rule that only the person holding the Mace can speak.
4 Notes of who speaks may be taken either simply as a list of names or by drawing lines on a diagram of the people sitting in the group. E.g.

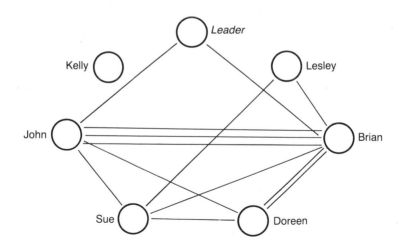

5 After stopping the game show them the record of where the Mace has gone. Ask the group:

- *what does this tell you about the importance of different members of the group?*

In the group illustrated this question might be directed to Kelly first to avoid her being excluded altogether and then to the others who said least. The importance of their contribution at this stage can be stressed as they have been in the best position to observe. Also ask:

- *is your participation typical of the way you behave in other groups?*
- *are you happy with your participation in this group or do you want to change it?*

THE MOUSE THAT TURNS

Materials: Pens and paper. Container as a ballot box. Copies of elected leader's briefing sheet on page 118.

Time: 45 minutes.

Procedure

1 In groups of 6 to 12 ask them to organize themselves into lines with the most important at the front and least important at the back. You will sometimes find people opt out to avoid conflict. It may ease the situation to point out that this is only the starting point of the game and that others may have their moment of power before it is ended. They are to write down their position in the line, starting from the first and most powerful person, who is 1, and the next, 2 . . .

2 Ask each group to form a circle and to discuss for 10 minutes, or until there is a natural pause:

- *how did you feel about the experience?*
- *where would you like to have ended up in the line?*
- *how important is it to be powerful in a group?*

3 Tell them:

You are now to elect someone you think will be a fair leader. The twist is that you will all have a different number of votes. You will all have the same number of votes as your position in the line-out.
    The first person will have only one vote, the fifth person five votes, and so on. These votes must be cast for one person only. Someone with several votes cannot divide them between two or more people.
    You have 2 minutes to decide who you are going to vote for.

4 Ask them to cast their votes into a hat, wastepaper bin, etc. Each ballot paper will have their position number on it which is also the number of votes that person has and the name of the person the votes are being cast for. Arrange for someone from another group to count the votes. They are not to reveal who voted for whom.

5 Give the elected leader his/her briefing sheet about a discussion he/she is to run with his/her own group. This will be focussed on:

- *how do you feel about the twist in the game which gave the power of voting to those who were originally seen as least powerful?*
- *what makes a fair leader?*
- *what do you think of the way I as the elected leader have run this group discussion?*

Variations
If there is any risk of bullying, greater precautions will be needed to make the election secret and the organizer will probably have to total the votes.

G4 THE MOUSE THAT TURNS – ELECTED LEADER'S BRIEFING SHEET

You are to run a discussion in your own group, especially about:

- how you feel about the twist in the game which gave the power of voting to those who were originally seen as least powerful?
- what makes a fair leader?
- what do the group feel about the way you have run the discussion?

118

Listening

Aims

1 To demonstrate that listening is not just a matter of sitting back and letting something happen. Effective listening requires activity by the listener.
2 Like all skills, listening can be improved with practice.

General comments

H1 **Rounds – I am going to Alaska** is an easier puzzle to solve than H2 **Rounds – London Bridge** but both are fairly light-hearted ways of demonstrating how selectively we listen. They have been used successfully with all ages.

H3 **Listening chain** shows how selective listening repeated several times in sequence results in considerable distortions of the original message. It is a development of the children's game Whispers where a short message is passed round the circle and comes back changed.

H4 **Listening in threes** involves both listening and summarizing skills. H5 **Paying attention** and its variations explore how the listener's posture and responses affect the speaker. Both these games are more complex in their procedures.

GAME	TIME	GROUP	MATERIALS
H1 ROUNDS - I AM GOING TO ALASKA	10-20 minutes	Up to 15	None
H2 ROUNDS - LONDON BRIDGE	10-20 minutes	Up to 15	None
H3 LISTENING CHAIN	2-3 minutes per person	Groups of 5-10	Listening chain Passage Instruction sheet
H4 LISTENING IN THREES	30 minutes	Groups of 3	None
H5 PAYING ATTENTION	10-15 minutes per round 45 minutes for a full rotation of turns	Groups of 3	Pens & paper

Other suitable games: A1 (variation 3), C4.

ROUNDS – I AM GOING TO ALASKA

Materials: None.

Time: 10–20 minutes.

Procedure

1 Sit the group in a circle and explain:

I am going to say a sentence which begins:

'My name is .... and I am going to Alaska and I am taking a ....* with me.'*

You are to repeat this but say your own name and the object you wish to take. I will tell you if you can or cannot take the object.
The aim of the game is to spot the rule which controls what you can or cannot take. If you spot it do not say what it is. I will give you a chance to tell other people whether they can or cannot take the object they have chosen with them.

2 The game begins by the leader saying:

'My name is .... and I am going to Alaska and I am taking a ....* with me. I can.'*

3 The next person is invited to repeat the formula adding his/her own name and object. If they both begin with the same initial the leader responds with *'You can'* but if not then *'You can't'*.

4 Keep on working round the group several times until everyone has spotted the rule or until the majority have done so. Get those who have spotted the rule to say 'You can' or 'You can't'.

5 Give clues if the game is in danger of dragging on. This game is a fun introduction to the idea of listening carefully and looking for patterns in what is said.

---

*Add own name and an object beginning with the same initial e.g. Katy can take a Kangaroo but not a husky.

ROUNDS – LONDON BRIDGE

Materials: None.

Time: 10–20 minutes.

Procedure

1 Sit the group in a circle and explain:

I am going to say a sentence which begins: 'I am going across London Bridge to . . . .' You are to repeat this in turn and add your own destination. I will tell you if you can or cannot. The aim of the game is to try to spot the rule which controls whether you can or cannot go. If you do spot it do not say what it is. You will be given a chance to tell other people whether they can or cannot.

2 The game begins by the leader saying:

I am going across London Bridge to – er – Durham and I can.

3 The next person is invited to repeat the phrase and add his/her own destination. If he/she includes an 'er' before the destination the leader responds *'You can'* but if not then *'You can't'*.

4 Keep on working round the group several times until everyone has spotted the rule. Get those who have spotted the rule to take over saying 'You can' or 'You can't'.

5 Make the 'er's' more obvious each time it's your go if the group is taking a long time to spot the rule. It is not easy to discover the rule because we do filter out things that seem unimportant when we are listening.

LISTENING CHAIN

Materials: Listening chain passage (pages 124–5). Copies of listening chain instruction sheet (pages 126–7).

Time: 2–3 minutes per person.

Procedure

1 Works best in groups of between 5 and 10. Select one of the two passages.
2 Explain:

I am going to send all of you out of hearing distance except for one person. I will read a passage to that person and he/she is to remember it and repeat it to the next person who I will call in. The second person will then repeat what he/she has been told to the third person and so on until everyone has had a turn.

After you have had a turn I will give you a form on which you can note what has been added to or left out of what you were told.

3 After this process has been completed, start a discussion on:

- what was left out?
- what was changed or even added?

You will usually find that names of places, numbers and anything unfamiliar is left out very quickly. Some words are misheard, e.g. 'castle' becomes 'cat'. If this happens the tendency is to change the story so that it still has some kind of sense. It has obvious implications for treating gossip with a healthy sense of doubt.
4 Read the passage to the whole group after they have given their observations during the discussion. Do not do this too early on or you will find their interest in the discussion can flag.

Variations

The passage can be chosen from a book or newspaper.

H3   LISTENING CHAIN

Read the instructions and one of these passages to the person who will start the listening chain.

'You are to listen to what I say and try to remember it. When I have finished reading this passage I will call in another person. You will tell that person everything you can remember. He/she will repeat this process with the next person and so on.'

A Night in the Lake District

We had been climbing all day and had been delayed by the poor weather. When we finally got to Coniston we found our bus had gone without us. We had been lucky to get a lift to Duddon Bridge. It was a welcome ten minutes out of the driving rain. Unfortunately no one seemed to be driving along the road to Seathwaite. After waiting a few minutes we started walking the five miles to our camp site.

As we walked the rain stopped but it had become very dark. The evening had become night. We could see car headlights in the distance. They were like snakes' eyes moving along the twisty fell roads. However none of them came past us.

After two hours walking we were only a few hundred yards from the camp. I was looking for the entrance on the left when Kay suddenly shouted. 'Look over there to the right. There are still people on top of that mountain.'

As I looked in the direction she pointed in I could see three torches moving in a straight line down from the summit of Caw. Sometimes the back two lights would stop and the first light would move ahead of them.

It would then stop and wait for the other two to catch up before they all moved off again.

On one occasion the first light seemed to move down a little and then climb back up again to the other lights. They all made a detour to the right before starting their descent again. We were glad we were not up there. It was the wrong time of day to be walking on the fells.

On the next day in the village shop, we discovered we had been watching a mountain rescue.

Each time the first light had moved ahead of the others the leader was trying to find his way down the many small crags which cover the mountain. He would climb to the bottom of a crag before the others would follow him. The time he climbed down and back up again was when he discovered he was at the top of a large quarry. If he had descended only a few more feet he would have fallen to his death. The shopkeeper who told us this thought the leader was lucky to be alive.

'It shows how dangerous the fells can be at night', he warned. 'Even if you are an experienced climber it is best to stay where you are when darkness falls and remain there until the morning. Better late in this world than early in the next.'

The Crash

Last Wednesday I was walking along Market Street to my dentist. I was half-way across the entrance to the fire station when the alarm sounded. Through the glass doors I could see men dashing about and blue lights flashing. As I ran out of the way I heard one of the engines start and there was a loud noise and the sound of breaking glass.

After running well clear of the entrance and away from the danger of being knocked down, I turned round. I was surprised to see the cab of one of the engines sticking through bent and broken doors. There was glass everywhere. Some of the glass came from the fire engine's broken headlights and windscreen. There was a great deal of shouting but no one seemed to be hurt. The fire engine must have rushed forward before the station doors had opened.

While all this was taking place I noticed a group of people standing behind me on the other side of the road. They were helping a motor-cyclist to his feet. As they moved to one side I could see a motor-bike on its side with its wheels still spinning. It was lying near the door of Jenny's Pie Shop. An old man was rubbing his leg and someone was helping him to sit down on a doorstep. I think the motor-cyclist must have swerved because he was watching the fire engine crash instead of watching the road ahead of him.

A few minutes later the firemen had forced open some other doors. A second fire engine set off at high speed towards the West End of the city.

I was ten minutes late when I got to the dentist's. He told me off but when he heard what had happened he did not seem too annoyed. Having two new fillings did not hurt any more than usual.

H3 LISTENING CHAIN – INSTRUCTION SHEET

Write down any changes that take place in the story compared to the way you were told it.

Speaker's name	Things missed out	Things added or changed
1		
2		
3		
4		
5		

6		
7		
8		
9		
10		

LISTENING IN THREES

Materials: None.

Time: 30 minutes.

Procedure

1 Divide the group into threes. Ask them to decide who is A, B and C. You can point out they will all have a turn at each of the three roles.
2 Instruct them:

A is to speak for 5 minutes on any subject that interests them, e.g. my favourite sport, the most exciting day of my life.

B waits for a natural break in what A is saying and then summarizes what has been said to C.

C makes a suitable comment or asks a question which helps to keep A's conversation flowing.

You will probably have to repeat these instructions several times before running the game.
3 After running the game for 5 minutes ask them to discuss:

- *Is B summarizing accurately and does C's response help A to keep going?*
- *If there are any problems with either of these, what could be done to improve the performance?*

4 Swap roles and repeat until everyone has had a turn at all the roles.
5 It is not unusual for people to find doing this exercise quite hard even after they have mastered the rules. This gives you the opportunity to emphasize that listening is a skill which is active because it involves making an effort; like other skills it improves with practice.

PAYING ATTENTION

Materials: Pens and paper.

Time: 10–15 minutes per round.

Procedure
1 Divide the group into threes and ask them to decide who is A, B and C.
2 Inform them:

A is to talk for 4 minutes about something that interests them, e.g. my favourite place, how I like to spend a weekend.

C is to observe what happens especially what B does and its effect on A. C may take notes.

For the first 2 minutes B is to look as bored as possible and is not to show any interest in what A says. I will tell you when the time is up.

For the last 2 minutes B is to look interested and to make helpful comments to encourage A to keep talking.

3 Run the game and inform them when 2 minutes and 4 minutes are up.
4 Ask them to discuss:

- What made it hard for the talker?
- What made it seem easier for the talker especially what postures did the listener take that helped?

Variations
Instead of suggesting boredom publicly you could distribute cards to the listeners which must not be shown to anyone else. These would then describe the role to be taken by the listener. For example:

Bored   There's nothing you can say to interest me.
Big-head   Anything you can do I can do better.
Worrier   Everything you say makes me anxious.
Know-all   I know just what you mean even before you say it.
Depressed Oh dear, how sad.

The game runs in the same way with 2 minutes following the role on the card and 2 minutes helping. The final discussion would include:

- What does the speaker think the listener has on the card?
- What feelings the listener's behaviour arouse in the speaker?

Asking questions

Aims

1 To increase questioning skills as a means of gathering information.
2 To distinguish between open and closed questions and their appropriate uses.

General comments

I1 **Who am I?** I2 **Shapes** and I3 **Samaritans** all use closed questions exclusively. These are questions which expect only a one-word answer, usually 'yes' or 'no'. All the games show how difficult it is to obtain a complete answer about a complex situation if only closed questions are used. The effectiveness depends on the order of the closed questions and working from the general to the specific. This is an important skill in designing flow charts and some computer programs.

I4 **Question swapshop** can be used as the lead into a discussion about the use of particular types of questions or as a fun way of introducing people to each other.

I5 **Radio interview** and I6 **The job interview (variation)** look at when open questions are more appropriate than closed questions. Generally people have difficulty in phrasing their questions as open questions which expect an answer of more than one word. This is particularly obvious when an untrained person is asked to become an interviewer. Asking open questions is a skill which has wide applications and is particularly useful to receptionists and people who work behind counters or who deal with the public. They are particularly useful when the questioner has little idea of the likely answer or in situations where the focus of attention or interest is on the person giving the answer.

GAME	TIME	GROUP	MATERIALS
I1 WHO AM I?	3 minutes per person	5-10 people	Pens, paper and sticky tape
I2 SHAPES	20 minutes	Pairs	Pens and paper Blackboard/ flipchart
I3 SAMARITANS	20-30 minutes	Pairs	Pens and paper Chairs
I4 QUESTION SWAPSHOP	About 45 minutes	Pairs	Pens and paper optional
I5 RADIO INTERVIEW	40 minutes	Threes	Pens and paper for observer Copies of instruction sheet
I6 JOB INTERVIEW (Variation)	45 minutes - 1 hour	Fours	Pens and paper Copies of instruction sheet from C3 for the applicant and the interviewer Copies of I5 observer instruction sheets

WHO AM I?

Materials: Pens, paper and sticky tape for labels to be stuck on the back of someone.

Time: About 3 minutes per person.

Procedure

1 On the labels write down the names of famous people who are likely to be known to the group, e.g. pop stars, sports personalities, film and TV characters or personalities.
2 Pin one of these to the back of someone in the group without him/her seeing it. The label is shown to the rest of the group by that person turning round slowly.
3 The person wearing the label has to try to find out the name written on it by asking questions which can be answered only 'yes' or 'no'.
4 After everyone has had a go, ask:

- *how difficult was it asking only questions which received the answer 'yes' or 'no'?*
- *are there other types of questions you might have used which would have made the process easier?*

This could lead on to the use of open questions which expect an answer of more than one word and usually begin with 'how', 'why', 'what', 'where', etc.

Variations

Get each member of the group to secretly write down the name of a famous person and shuffle the labels before starting the game.

SHAPES

Materials: Pens and paper. Blackboard or flipchart to give example.

Time: 20 minutes.

Procedure

1 Explain:

> *You are to divide into pairs and sit back to back. One of you will draw a pattern using squares, rectangles, triangles and circles. You cannot use more than eight separate shapes, e.g.*

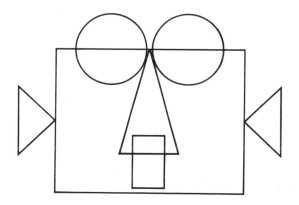

> *The other person is not allowed to see it. Their task is to try to redraw it by asking questions to which you can answer only 'yes' or 'no'.*
>
> *You have a maximum of 5 minutes and then you swap over roles.*
>
> *At the end of the game you compare the original drawings with the copies.*

2 After this process has been carried out, ask them to join the pair nearest to them. In fours they are to discuss:

- which questions were most helpful in getting correct information?
- did the order of the questions matter?

Variations

1 Instead of drawing shapes one person could hold an object and the other try to discover what it is.
2 K1 **Draw this ...** is a variation of this which focusses on giving clear information as well as questioning. It also provides a different way of organizing the exercise.

13

SAMARITANS

Materials: Pens and paper. Chairs to sit on.

Time: 20–30 minutes.

Procedure

1 Divide the group into pairs. Ask them to sit on chairs with their backs to each other. They should be sitting close enough to allow them to communicate by tapping on the back of the chair.

2 Ask them to think of a problem someone might phone the Samaritans about. One of the pair will pretend to be this person and as the other person has to guess the problem, so it should not be too complex. They can change their age, sex and nationality if they want to. The problems might be family, personal, financial or legal. They are to write the problem down but they should keep it secret at this stage.

3 Explain:

Telephone counselling services often receive silent calls. Sometimes before someone is willing to speak they go through a stage where they will only tap the phone. This game recreates that situation. You will each have a turn of pretending to be the caller who will remain silent. The answers to questions are given by tapping on the back of your partner's chair: one tap for 'yes', two taps for 'no'.

The questioner will need to be quite skilled to discover the problem. It is easier if you set out establishing the sex and the age of the person and then the broad type of the problem, e.g. family, personal, financial or legal, and then work towards the details. You will need to word your questions so that they can be answered 'yes' or 'no'.

At the end of 5 minutes I will stop you and ask the tapper to show the questioner the problem they have written down. You will then swap roles.

4 At the end of the game ask:

- *how difficult was it to discover the problem?*
- *how did you feel as the questioner about being able to ask only questions which could receive one-word answers?*

● *was there anything the tapper really wanted to say but could not? If so, what?*

Variations

1 The discussion can continue with looking at the types of problem offered by the tappers. This would be particularly appropriate if the game is part of a sequence looking at helping skills, prejudice or stigma.

2 For younger groups it may be more appropriate if they substitute drawing an object they would like to own for the personal problem. Otherwise the rules remain the same.

14

QUESTION SWAPSHOP

Materials: Pens and paper for note taking are optional.

Time: About 45 minutes.

Procedure

1 Each person is to find someone they do not know very well and form a pair.
2 Tell them:

Each of you is to be given a choice of how you are to be introduced to the rest of the group. You are to choose the six questions you would most like to be asked by the other person, who will report your answers to the others. Tell your partner what these questions are. There is no need to reveal the answers at this stage. You have approximately ten minutes to remember the six questions chosen by your partner.

3 When they have completed this, ask them to change partners and find someone else who they do not know very well.
4 Tell them:

Point out your original partner and make sure the person you are paired with now knows who that was. Tell your partner the questions that person would like to be asked.

5 When everyone has completed this instruct them:

Each of you is to approach the person who has just been pointed out to you to quiz them with the questions they would like to be asked.

This will involve milling around which is part of the fun.

6 If the group is less than ten bring them back into a circle and ask them to introduce the person they have just questioned to the rest of the group.

If the group is larger than ten ask them to approach the first person they see not talking to someone. They are to point out the person they have just questioned and they are to relate that person's answers. When both have done this, they are to move on to someone else until you call time.

7 End with a general discussion.

RADIO INTERVIEW

Materials: Pen and paper for the observer. Copies of the instruction sheet (pages 140–1).

Time: 40 minutes.

Procedure

1 Explain:

You are to divide into groups of three. Each of you will have a turn at being a radio interviewer, the person being interviewed and an observer.

One of the things radio interviewers are trained to do is to avoid asking questions which expect one-word answers. This gives the person being interviewed more time to give their point of view and gives the interviewer time to think of a follow-up question.

Decide who is A, B and C. Give them time to do this.

A is the person being interviewed and must think of a topic or interest to be asked questions about. This might be a favourite hobby or place, or some strongly held view about politics, blood sports, strikes, etc. A is to tell B what the topic is.

B is the interviewer and you have 3 minutes to think of questions which will encourage A to talk. Every time you get a one-word answer, C will make a note of it. C will also note down the words of every question that gets an answer. Generally if you begin your questions with 'how', 'what', 'why', 'where', 'when', you will get answers of several words.

2 Distribute instruction sheets to each person.
3 Give B 3 minutes to prepare his/her questions.
4 Run the game for 5 minutes. Rotate the roles and repeat procedures 3 and 4 twice to give everyone a turn.
5 During a discussion ask them to consider when they would use open and closed questions.

I5 RADIO INTERVIEW INSTRUCTION SHEET

A. PERSON BEING INTERVIEWED

1 Think of a topic you are interested in and are willing to be asked questions about, e.g. a favourite hobby, place or some strongly held views about politics, bloodsports, strikes, etc.

2 When you have decided on a topic tell B, who is going to interview you for radio, what the topic is to be.

3 You will then have 2 or 3 minutes to think of answers to the questions the radio interviewer might ask.

4 You will be interviewed when the leader tells you to start.

B THE RADIO INTERVIEWER

1 You are a radio interviewer who is to interview A about a topic he will tell you the title of.

2 After A has told you the topic he has chosen you have 3 minutes to plan your questions. You should try to use open questions which produce a more than one-word answer. These questions often start with the words 'how', 'why', 'what', 'when', etc. You should avoid closed questions which produce only one-word answers as these give you very little time to think of your next question.

3 When you are interviewing listen to what A says and try to produce questions which follow on as naturally as possible.

4 Interview A when the leader tells you to start.

C OBSERVER

1 The other two members of your group are going to act out a radio interview. They will have a few minutes to prepare for this.

2 When the interview starts you are to make a note of every question that results in a one-word answer. Take just enough notes to help you remember the question otherwise you will miss what happens next.

THE JOB INTERVIEW (variation)

Materials: Pens and paper. Copies of the interviewer and applicant instruction sheets from C3 **The job interview**, and observer instruction sheets on pages 78–81 and 143–5.

Time: 45 minutes to 1 hour.

Procedure
The same as C3 **The job interview** except that the observers receive different instruction sheets. The observer assisting the interviewer will concentrate on questioning skills during the role play. The observer helping the applicant will concentrate on the skills of selling oneself.

16 THE JOB INTERVIEW (variation) – OBSERVER INSTRUCTION SHEET: SELLING ONESELF

1 PREPARATION STAGE

You are to ask the person playing the applicant:

- *what kind of job do you want to apply for?*
- *what do you expect to do in that kind of job?*

Encourage the applicant to be as realistic as possible. It should be the sort of job they would apply for if they saw a vacancy advertised. If the answer is a long one you may wish to take notes.

Pass this information on to the person playing the interviewer. *The applicant and the interviewer should not talk to each other at this stage.* They will be given 10 minutes to prepare for the interview.

You are to assist the applicant to prepare for the questions which are likely to be asked at an interview. Encourage the applicant to treat the situation as realistically as possible.

2 THE INTERVIEW

During the interview you should sit quietly to one side where you can hear what is being said. Do not interrupt them.

You are to observe what happens and take notes to help you answer the following points:

a *Did the applicant's answers seem to be the kind that would be given in a real interview?*

b *What did the applicant say which seemed most likely to improve the chance of being employed?*

c *How did the applicant and interviewer sit during the interview? Did the posture he/she took suggest interest or boredom? Did the posture he/she took suggest interest or boredom? (Be prepared to imitate the postures when you explain your answer.)*

d *Is there anything the applicant could do to sell him/herself more?*

16 THE JOB INTERVIEW (variation) – OBSERVER INSTRUCTION SHEET: QUESTIONING SKILLS

1 PREPARATION STAGE

You will work with the interviewer.

The other observer will ask the person playing the applicant:

- *what kind of job do you want to apply for?*
- *what do you expect to do in that kind of job?*

This information will be passed to the interviewer through the applicant's observer. *The applicant and the interviewer should not talk to each other at this stage.* They will be given 10 minutes to prepare for the interview.

You are to assist the interviewer to choose the sort of questions which will draw out as much information as possible from the applicant.

2 THE INTERVIEW

During the interview you should sit quietly to one side where you can hear what is being said. Do not interrupt them.

You are to observe what happens, keep count of the two types of questions and take notes to help you answer the following points:

a *Count the number of open and closed questions the interviewer uses.*

Open questions expect more than a one-word answer and often start with words like 'how', 'why', 'what', 'when', 'where', e.g. 'How did you come here?'

Closed questions expect a one-word answer, usually 'yes' or 'no', e.g. 'Did you walk here?'

	Place a mark in this column for each question asked	Total numbers
Closed questions		
Open questions		

b Do you think the interviewer would have got more information by using more open or closed questions? If so, when?

c Which of the interviewer's questions seemed most likely to be used in a real interview?

d Which of the interviewer's questions seemed to encourage the applicant to speak most?

e Give examples of the questions you would have liked to have asked if you had been the interviewer.

Non-verbal communication

Aims

1 To draw attention to the amount of information we convey non-verbally.
2 To introduce the main ways we communicate non-verbally.

General comments

How we behave non-verbally is an important means of communication and can confirm or discredit what we say.

J1 **Round – North Pole** and J2 **Killer** are both fun games which draw attention to the main areas of the body we use to communicate moods and attitudes.

J3 **Headbands** allows individuals to consider how much information about the way others see us is picked up from their non-verbal communication.

J4 **Observer** encourages feedback about the participants' non-verbal behaviour.

J5 **Moods** looks at what aspects of non-verbal behaviour signal particular moods.

GAME	TIME	GROUP	MATERIALS
J1 ROUND – NORTH POLE	15 minutes	Up to 15	None
J2 KILLER	10 minutes or more	Up to 12	Prepared pieces of folded paper
J3 HEADBANDS	20 minutes	Up to 12	Pens, paper and string
J4 OBSERVER	40 minutes	Threes	Pens and paper
J5 MOODS	15-30 minutes	Any size	Prepared cards

Other suitable games: G1, M1.

ROUND – NORTH POLE

Materials: None.

Time: 15 minutes.

Procedure

1 Sit the group in a circle and explain:

We are all going to use the phrase:

'When I went to the North Pole I found a . . .'

You will invent what you found and I will tell you whether 'You did' or 'You didn't'. You are to try to spot the rule behind my decision. If you do discover it don't tell anyone until the end of the game. I may give you a turn at saying 'You did' or 'You didn't'.

2 Leader starts by crossing his/her legs and says:

'When I went to the North Pole I found a tent. I did.'

The next person in the circle then has a turn and so on. The leader responds 'You did' only if they have their legs crossed.

3 If the game starts going on too long give clues by exaggerated crossing and uncrossing legs.

4 This game can be used just as light relief or to make a point about non-verbal communication.

One of the reasons why it is hard to spot the rule about crossed legs is that it is often done in public situations. This may be partly because it is considered polite but also because it is a comforting activity, as is folding one's arms. In a group game such as this people tend to be slightly anxious, so it is not surprising if they seek comfort by crossing their legs. It is not consciously noticed unless looked for.

Variations

Use folded arms instead of crossed legs.

KILLER

Materials: Enough pieces of folded paper for the whole group. Only one of these is marked with a capital 'M'.

Time: 10 minutes or longer.

Procedure

1 Arrange the group in a circle so that they can all see each other.
2 Inform them that you are going to distribute folded pieces of paper. They are **not** to show these to each other. Only one person will receive one marked with a capital 'M'. This person is a murderer. The way that they will kill someone is by winking at them. The person who is winked at need not die immediately but must die within 30 seconds. They show they are dead by shutting their eyes or falling down. It is for everyone who has not been winked at to try to guess who the murderer is.

   If the group is inclined to make so many guesses that the murderer has no chance, then a further rule may be added that each person has only two guesses.

   The murderer is to kill as many people as possible before being spotted.
3 The game can be used just as light relief and fun but it can also be used to draw attention to the way people use their eyes to communicate with each other.

This point can be emphasized by asking them to stare into their neighbour's eyes for 60 seconds and then ask:

- *what did you feel about the experience?*
- *what does the person who looks away first feel about the other person?*

Usually they will say they felt they had lost or given in. Averting one's eyes from the look of someone else is a signal of submission or non-aggression.

HEADBANDS

Materials: Pen, paper and string to make headbands.

Time: 20 minutes.

Procedure

1 Prepare enough headbands for all the people in the group. Each headband should have written on it a mood or attitude (see examples below).
2 Tie a headband to each person. It should be facing forwards. The person wearing the headband should not see what is written on it.
3 Arrange the group in a circle. Ask them to pretend that they are about to go on a weekend camp together and they are to discuss the arrangements, e.g. where they will go and what they will do.

   They are to react to everyone according to the label on that person's forehead. They are not to say what the label is.
4 Allow the discussion to go on for 5–10 minutes, then ask them:

   - *what do you think is written on your headband?*
   - *how do you know?*
   - *did it affect the way people reacted to you non-verbally, e.g. their movements and postures?*

Variations

Instead of forming a discussion group they can mill around together not speaking but reacting to each other's labels non-verbally.

EXAMPLES

BAD TEMPERED   CARING PERSON
VERY FUNNY PERSON   GOOD SPORT
BULLY   PRACTICAL JOKER
DEPRESSED   RELIABLE
FRIENDLY   BORING
LEADER   LIAR
SHY

OBSERVER

Materials: Pens and paper.

Time: 40 minutes.

Procedure

1 Divide the group into threes. Ask them to decide who is A, B and C.
2 Explain:

This is a game where A talks to B about the most interesting thing that has happened to him/her in the last year. B can ask questions and should try to encourage A.

C is the observer and may take notes. C is to watch the postures and mannerisms of A and B. After a 5-minute discussion C will tell A and B what has happened and should be willing to imitate their movements and the way they sat.

Everyone will have a turn at each role.

3 Bring the group back together and discuss:

● *what postures did the listener take which encouraged the speaker to keep talking?*
● *what did the speakers do to show how they felt about what they were talking about?*

Variations

The observer could be asked to take particular note of when people look at each other and when they look away.

MOODS

Materials: Prepared cards.

Time: 15–30 minutes.

Procedure

1 Arrange the group in a circle. They will be working in pairs.
2 Distribute to each pair a card with a mood written on it, e.g. Angry, Afraid, In Love, Tired, Broken Hearted, Excited, Victorious, Hunted, Mad, Depressed.
   They are to keep what is written on the card to themselves.
3 Each pair will have a turn in the circle. One person will be the dummy and the other will arrange their legs, hands and face to demonstrate the mood on their card. This process will be completed before the group begins to guess which mood is being portrayed.

Giving and receiving feedback

Aims

1 To develop skills in the giving and receiving of useful feedback.
2 To provide a safe environment to practise these skills.

General comments

'Feedback' is an alternative word for 'criticism'. Unfortunately the word 'criticism' so often means a damning statement that we put up our emotional defences at the mere mention of the word and it is hard to give it positive meaning.

The best ways of giving and receiving feedback are explained on page 20.

K1 **Draw this . .**, K2 **Something in common** and K3 **Tangrams** all draw attention to the importance of expressing oneself clearly in the game. They provide opportunities for feedback in the discussions.

K4 **The message of happiness** encourages the use of the skills in giving feedback in a non-threatening way because it focusses on liked behaviour.

K5 **The bad and the good** and K6 **Computer** involve giving feedback about both liked and disliked behaviour. This is less threatening in K6 **Computer** because they do not have to invent the feedback; it is supplied to them on cards. When K5 **The bad and the good** is used it is especially important to give sufficient time for the participants to check out what has been said and to discuss the experience.

GAME	TIME	GROUP	MATERIALS
K1 DRAW THIS ...	20 minutes	Any size	Pens and paper Blackboard/ flipchart
K2 SOMETHING IN COMMON	10-30 minutes	5-6	Pens and paper Prepared cards Chairs
K3 TANGRAMS	$1\frac{1}{2}$ hours	Groups of 5-8 including observers	Cardboard pieces in envelopes Copies of instruction sheets Pens and paper
K4 THE MESSAGE OF HAPPINESS	15 minutes	Groups of up to 10	Pens and paper
K5 THE BAD AND THE GOOD	About 2-3 minutes/person	Groups of up to 12	None
K6 COMPUTER	About 30 minutes	Any size	Prepared sheets

Other suitable games: P1, P2, P4.

DRAW THIS . . .

Materials: Pens and paper. Blackboard or flipchart to give example.

Time: 20 minutes.

Procedure

1 Organize the group so that they are sitting facing the blackboard or flipchart.
2 Two or more members of the circle are to turn round so that they cannot see each other's drawings or the blackboard/flipchart.
3 One member of the group is to draw a pattern of circles, squares, triangles, etc. on the blackboard. It must use at least five shapes which may overlap. E.g.

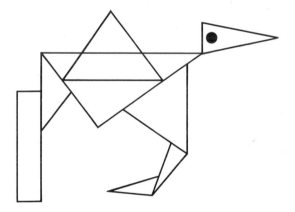

4 Either the drawer or another member of the group is asked to describe what is on the blackboard and to help those facing the outside of their circle to reproduce it exactly. The speaker may not look at their drawings until he/she is satisfied that they have finished drawing. The drawers may ask questions at any stage.
5 Other members of the group act as observers and once the attempt at reproducing the original drawing is over they should be asked:

- *how far do the original and the copies match?*
- *what instructions led to errors being made?*
- *how could those instructions have been better phrased or ordered?*

These observations can form the basis of a group discussion which can include feedback on what the speakers have achieved or how they can improve.

Variations
See 12 **Shapes** for organizing this exercise in pairs rather than in front of the whole group.

SOMETHING IN COMMON

Materials: Pens and paper for each member. Cards completed from examples on pages 158–9. Chairs arranged in a tight circle and facing outwards, e.g.

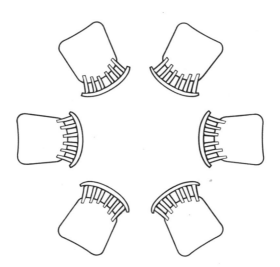

Time: 10–30 minutes.

Procedure

1 Ask everyone to take a seat. From now onwards they cannot talk or turn towards anyone.
2 Explain:

You will each be given a card with five numbers on it. All the cards have only one other thing in common. You are to try to discover what this is, but

- *you cannot speak or turn to anyone;*
- *you cannot show your card to anyone;*
- *you may communicate by writing notes to each other;*

- no written note can have more than three numbers on it. This rule
  still applies whether or not the numbers are written as words or
  symbols.*

You can repeat the instructions and answer questions about them but
do not interpret them.

3 Withdraw the last instruction marked* if the group is struggling to find
  the solution.

4 After the group has found the solution, lead a discussion on:

- how did you feel during the game?
- how did not being able to speak affect you?
- which notes were particularly helpful? Were there any notes you
  could not understand?
- did you feel anyone opted out of the game?
- did anyone take charge of the game?
- if you were faced with the same kind of problem again, what would
  you do differently?

Variations

1 To make the game easier draw five dominoes on the cards so that the
  only thing in common is no card contains a '6'. (Missing out any other
  number makes it easier but leaving out the blank is the hardest version
  of this variation.)

2 Use a pack of cards and remove one suite. Shuffle the cards and then
  place five cards in an envelope for each group member. Discard the
  remaining cards.

3 Change the numbers to make it easier or harder but include false clues,
  e.g. one number the same on all the cards except one, some numbers
  going up in series.

Solutions

Set one: The difference between the first and last numbers is 7.

Set two: All the cards contain 9 digits.

157

K2 SOMETHING IN COMMON – SAMPLE CARDS

Set one

7	10	21	17	14

18	11	8	16	25

28	1	14	34	35

39	32	8	14	46

44	14	1	9	51

45	14	8	23	52

Set two

63	21	6	12	36

3362	0	33	6	2

6	12	24	48	96

33	6	132	9	66

4	8	5280	36	3

26	3	103	6	52

TANGRAMS

Materials: Cardboard pieces in envelopes. Copies of instruction sheet on pages 162–75. Pens and paper.

Time: 1½ hours.

Procedure

1 Before starting the game and out of sight of the participants divide the 14 pieces as evenly as possible into 4 or 6 envelopes depending on the number of participants in each group. Number the envelopes and the pieces on both sides with the same number. This is important as after the preparation stage the pieces have to be returned to their original envelopes.
2 Divide the group into two teams A and B of 4–6 participants and additional observer(s).
3 Explain:

There are three stages to this game:

The planning stage
I will give each of the participants an envelope with cardboard shapes in it. You will also be given a silhouette of two or three shapes you are to make from the pieces. These silhouettes are to scale.

After you have worked out the puzzle you are to decide how to tell another group, who have not seen the puzzle before, how to solve it. Your aim is to make your instructions so clear that they can solve the puzzle more quickly than you did yourself.

You have 20 minutes for this preparation stage. At the end of the time I will ask you to put the pieces back in the envelopes.

The instruction stage
You will move away from the table and the new group will sit down. Without showing them any plans or using marked pieces you will instruct them in the way previously agreed by your group on how to complete the puzzle as quickly as possible. All the pieces stay in the envelopes during this stage. You have up to a maximum of 10 minutes.

The construction stage

The new group will construct the two shapes as quickly as possible.

The observers will observe all three stages and their comments will form the basis of our discussion afterwards.

4 Run the game. At the change-over from the preparation stage to the instruction stage move group A to B's table and ask B to instruct them. After group A have constructed the puzzles move group B to A's table.

5 Bring all the participants and observers together for a discussion based on working through the observers' comments. Encourage attempts at feedback which are specific and positive.

Variations

Two sets of puzzles are provided. The *birds* are easier to solve than the *shapes*. Both puzzles can be further simplified by making the cardboard pieces for each object a different colour.

Instructions for preparing the material for K3 Tangrams

1 Photostat pages 166–7.

2 Join the box lines so that A meets B and C meets D.

K3 TANGRAMS – PARTICIPANTS' INSTRUCTION SHEET

Planning stage: 20 minutes

1 You have been given an envelope containing cardboard pieces and the plans of two or three shapes you are to construct. The plans are to scale. There is only one possible solution.

2 You are to discover the solution and may take notes to draw on the plan.

3 You are to work out how to instruct a group of people who have not seen this puzzle before how to solve it more quickly than you did.

- You may not show them any plans, drawings or notes you have made.
- You may not mark any of the pieces.

4 At the end of this stage you will replace the pieces in their original envelopes.

Instruction stage: up to 10 minutes maximum

Tell the new group how they are to solve the puzzle in the quickest possible time. They cannot take the pieces out of the envelopes. You may not show them any plans, drawings or notes you have made.

Construction stage: no time limit

Planners and instructors

You will stand away from the table and observe how far your instructions help or hinder finding a solution.

Constructors

You will solve the puzzle in the quickest possible time. You are to create the objects on your plans from the shapes in your envelopes. The plans are to scale.

K3 TANGRAMS — OBSERVER INSTRUCTION SHEET

You are not to participate in the game or talk to those who are doing so.

You will watch a team go through the stages of solving a puzzle and then planning how to instruct a new group on how to solve it as quickly as possible. They will instruct the new group. The new group will then solve the puzzle.

Planning stage: 20 minutes

Start time:		
Time spent solving puzzle:		
Time spent planning instructions:		

1 Do they all take part equally?

2 Does/do leader(s) emerge? How do they treat the group? Does the leadership change?

3 Does anyone play a major part in solving the puzzle?

4 How do they use their own experience of solving the puzzle in planning their instructions?

5 Is there anything you have noticed which seems to be particularly helping or hindering their attempts to plan their instructions?

6 Do the same people who played important roles in solving the puzzle play as important a role in planning the instructions?

Instruction stage: up to 10 minutes maximum

1 Who is involved in giving the instructions?

2 How do these differ from what was agreed earlier?

3 Do the group who is being instructed ask questions? How are these answered?

Construction stage:

Time started:	
Time completed:	
Total time:	

1 Do they all take part equally?

2 Does/do leader(s) emerge? How do they treat the group? Does the leadership change?

3 How far do they follow the instructions given to them? Is there a time when they begin to try to find their own solution?

4 Which instructions were helpful and were understood?

5 Did any instructions seem to confuse those following them?

K3 TANGRAMS – MAKING THE PIECES

1 Copy this plan on to cardboard joining A to B and C to D. Then cut out the shapes.

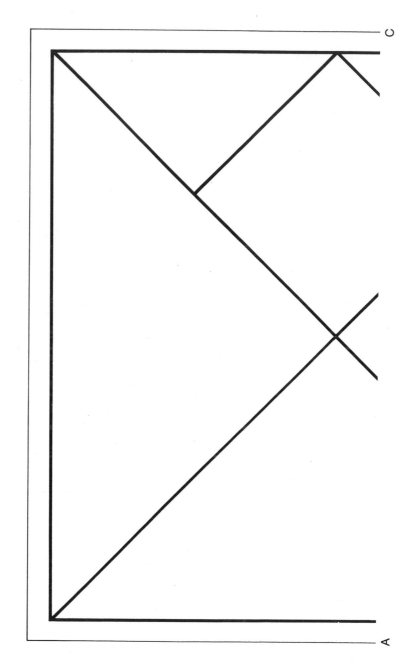

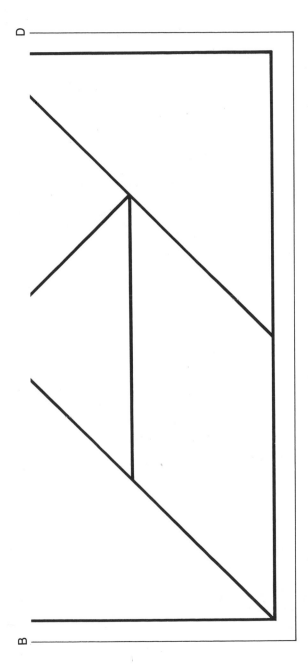

2 *Each team will need two sets of pieces (14 pieces in all). These should be mixed together and shared out equally between the envelopes* – one envelope for each participant.

Mark each envelope and both sides of the pieces in it with the same number so that the pieces can be returned to the same envelope at the end of the planning stage.

K3 TANGRAMS – BIRDS PUZZLE

Using the shapes you have been given you are to make two birds which have the same shape as these silhouettes.

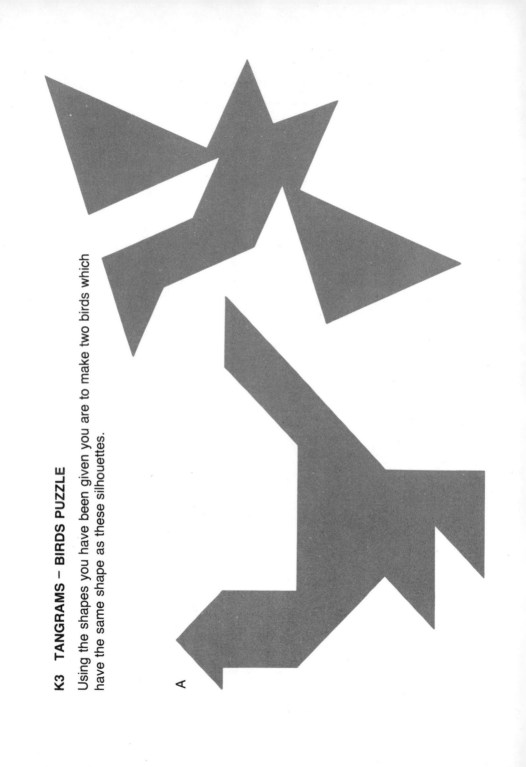

A

K3 TANGRAMS – BIRDS PUZZLE

B

The shapes you make must be three times larger than these.

K3 TANGRAMS – SHAPES PUZZLE

You are to make these shapes from the pieces you have been given.
These silhouettes are not actual size but they are drawn to scale.

A

K3 TANGRAMS – SHAPES PUZZLE

B

A

K3 TANGRAMS – BIRDS PUZZLE

B

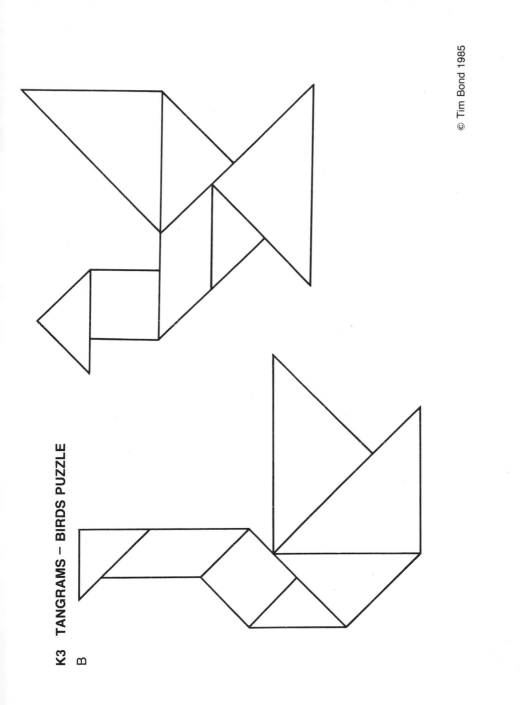

Solutions

A

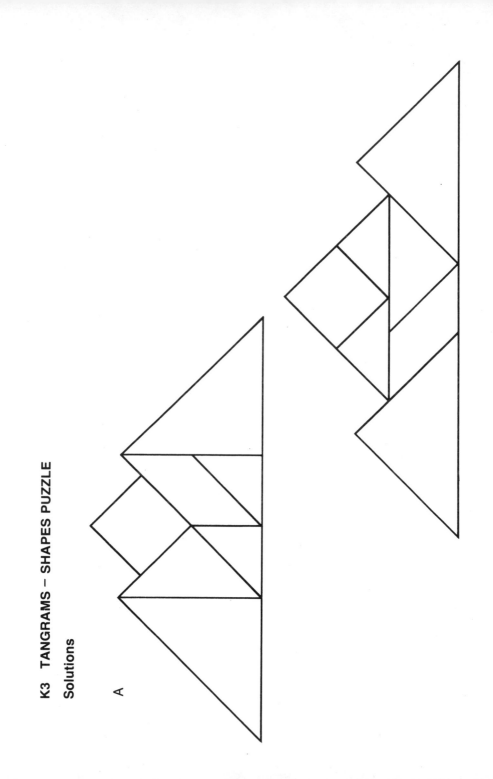

B

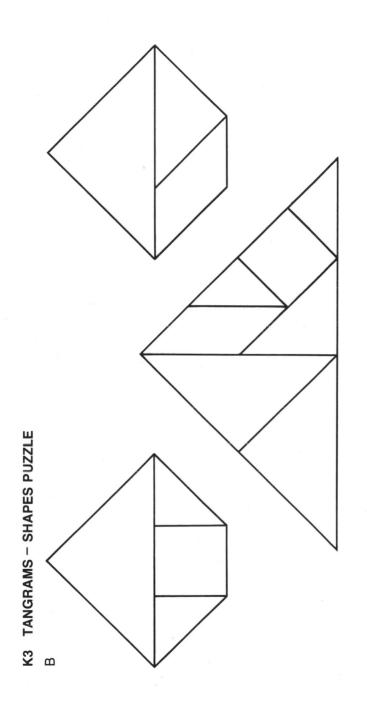

THE MESSAGE OF HAPPINESS

Materials: Pens and paper.

Time: 15 minutes.

Procedure

1 Explain:

You are to write a message to each person in the group saying what it is you like best about that person or how they make you happier.

- *Try to make each message something which could apply only to that person.*
- *The message should be as specific as possible so if you think someone is friendly give examples of what they do, e.g. that they smile at everyone or mention a particular incident.*
- *Begin each message with the other person's name and then the words, 'I like . . .'*

When you have written the message, sign your name, fold the paper and put the name of the person it is for on the outside.

After everyone has written their messages we will then exchange them with the people they are intended for.

THE BAD AND THE GOOD

Materials: None.

Time: About 2–3 minutes per person.

Procedure

1 This game works only within groups where there is already a high degree of trust. There is a slight risk that someone may be upset by the bad that they hear about themselves. The leader should be prepared to listen to their statements about how they feel; he/she requires both sensitivity and honesty to help the game succeed. The leader should be a participant, otherwise the group members will feel able to opt out.

2 Explain:

Each person is going to say one thing they don't like and one thing they do like about the person on their left.
   Both statements should:

- *be honest. This is most important;*
- *refer to something the other person can do something about or within their control, e.g. not a scar or mole but something they can change like putting their hand in front of their mouth when they speak.*

The person receiving the statements of the bad and the good:

- *can ask questions to make sure that what is being said is understood. This checking out is important;*
- *should listen to both the bad and the good. The tendency is not to hear the good but this is also an important statement about that person.*

3 Give the group a few minutes to think of what to say. Either ask for a volunteer to start or the leader can start. The leader's contribution will often determine the quality of other people's contributions. 'I would like you better if you weren't so pushy' is less helpful, because it does not describe the specific behaviour, than 'I would like you better if you didn't keep shouting everyone down.' Similarly 'I like your enthusiasm' can be re-expressed 'I like the way you always want to take part. It

encourages me to do the same', which is a full explanation of the behaviour and its effect.

4 After everyone has had a turn, point out that if anyone is in doubt about what has been said this is an opportunity to check it out. If they have already done so and are upset they may wish to discuss it with other members of the group or with the leader afterwards.

Variations

The bad and the good statements are written down and a similar procedure to K4 **The message of happiness** is used.

COMPUTER

Materials: Prepared cards (see pages 180–1).

Time: 30 minutes or more.

Procedure

1 The group needs to know each other well or at least well enough to be able to know who to give the cards to. The content of the cards must be appropriate to their level of knowledge of each other.
2 Arrange the group in a circle with the pile of cards face down in the centre.
3 Explain:

In the pile are some nice statements about people and some not so nice. In this game someone will pick up a card, read it and hand it to the person it most applies to. The person receiving the card will read out what it says. (For less experienced groups it is better if they keep the content of the card to themselves.) He/she will then take another card from the pile and give it to the most appropriate person. You may keep the cards you receive until the end of the game.

4 Run the game until the pile of cards is exhausted.
5 Be prepared for having to reveal your own feelings about members of the group as well as receiving their views of you.

It is possible someone may not receive any cards. This may be because none of the cards are appropriate to that person. If the person is new to the group then it may be because the others do not know him/her yet.

EXAMPLES FOR CARDS

Suitable for all levels of groups:

The most considerate person.

The person with the most expressive face.

The person who smiles the most.

The person with the nicest eyes.

The happiest person.

The person you would most like to know better.

The person who tries hardest.

The kindest person.

The best dressed person.

The saddest person.

The person who moans most.

The cheekiest person.

The most affectionate person.

The busiest person.

The person who seems the same all the time.

The most trustworthy person.

The person who makes me laugh.

The person with the knobbliest knees.

The most serious person.

The cuddliest person.

The most kissable person.

The quietest person.

The silliest person.

The bravest person.

The easiest person to talk to.

Suitable additional cards for groups whose members know each other well:

The person who sulks most.

The most annoying person.

The person who gets missed out.

The person who ought to be encouraged the most.

The biggest scrounger.

The person you would most like to work with.

The bossiest person.

The person who loses his/her temper most easily.

The most honest person.

The most ambitious person.

The person best in control of his/her temper.

The person who takes the most risks.

The sexiest person.

The most level headed person.

The person you would like to go on holiday with.

The person who makes the best of things.

The person who has made the best impression on you.

The calmest person.

The biggest eater.

The laziest person.

The most untrustworthy person.

The most serious person.

The person who talks about sex most.

The most critical person.

The biggest gossip.

You can extend both these lists by asking groups for the things they would have liked to have had on the cards after they have played the game.

Barriers to communication

Aims

1 To explore the way preconceptions about what is said or done affect how we perceive it and can leave us with a wrong impression.
2 To look at behaviour in groups which prevents them functioning and distorts the communication.

General comments

If a person sees or hears something which is ambiguous or unclear the tendency is to try to interpret it in a way that is more familiar. This creates distortions in the communication of what has happened. L1 **The owl and the pussycat** and L2 **Washing the elephant** both create situations where the name of the game creates preconceptions in the minds of the participants. These preconceptions lead to results which surprise the group.

L3 **Escape** looks at the way prejudices influence decision making.

L4 **Saboteur** is more complicated to prepare than the others. It creates the expectation that there is a saboteur in the group and honest mistakes are misinterpreted. It is a cautionary experience which demonstrates not only the dangers of preconceptions (in this case created by the game) but also the tendency of groups to find a scapegoat to blame for difficulties which belong to the group and are not that person's fault. It is a game which works better with older people and requires a longer attention span by the participants.

- Games L1, L2 and L4 involve an element of deceiving the group to create the preconceptions. This may affect your relationship with the group.

- If you intend to use the same game again in the same agency you may wish to ask the participants not to reveal the twist in the game to other people. This is best done after the game(s).

GAME	TIME	GROUP	MATERIALS
L1 THE OWL AND THE PUSSYCAT	2 minutes for each person	6-12	Pen and paper Picture of the owl
L2 WASHING THE ELEPHANT	2 minutes for each person	6-10 for each run through	Blackboard/ flipchart
L3 ESCAPE	$1-1\frac{1}{2}$ hours	Groups of 6-10	Pens Instruction sheet Observer instruction sheet
L4 SABOTEUR	$1-1\frac{1}{2}$ hours	Groups of 6-8 plus one	Pens, rubbers and rules General instruction sheets Personal instructions Observer sheet Timekeeper sheet Maze plan Maze master copy Maze solution

Other suitable games: M2 (variation 3).

THE OWL AND THE PUSSYCAT

Materials: Picture of an owl (page 185) and blank paper and pencil for the group.

Time: 2 minutes for each group member.

Procedure

1 Write the name of the game in a prominent place before sending the whole group, except one, out of the room or at least out of sight of what is being done.
2 Show the one person left the drawing of the owl for about 30 seconds. Remove the drawing. Ask that person to redraw the picture from memory.
3 Call in the next person and show them the copy for 30 seconds, remove it and ask them to copy it from memory.
4 Keep on repeating this process. You may wish to continue to reduce the 30 seconds once the drawing has become simpler.
5 At the end of 6–8 copies the owl will have been transformed into something like a pussycat as drawn by children.

L1   THE OWL AND THE PUSSYCAT

Tracing of copy no. 9
Group members: adult residential social workers

WASHING THE ELEPHANT

Materials: Blackboard or flipchart. (Pens and paper for observers.*)

Time: About 2 minutes for each person.

Procedure

1 Draw attention to the name of the game by writing 'Washing the Elephant' on the blackboard or flipchart and explain to the group (between 6 and 10 people – the remainder may be observers):

We are going to play a game called Washing the Elephant. I will ask all but one of you to leave the room. I will show the person who remains a mime. He/she will call in the next person and repeat the mime in front of them. They will call in the next person and repeat the mime and so on until everyone has had a turn.

When you have had your turn you are to sit quietly (with any of the observers) and watch what happens. At the end of the game we will discuss any changes that have taken place and I will show you the original mime.*

2 After everyone except the first person (and the observers*) have moved out of sight and hearing, you explain:

The object of this game is to show how we interpret things which are not clear to us according to our own preconceptions. They are expecting Washing the Elephant but what I am going to mime is washing a car. We will wait and see how far the car turns into an elephant as the game proceeds.

3 Perform a mime of washing a car starting with filling the bucket and wringing out cloths. When washing the car pay particular attention to the wheels and the front and rear windows. The wheels will turn into legs and it is not uncommon for the windows to turn into a trunk and a tail. Be careful to walk round and not through the car.

4 Run the game. At the end ask what changes people saw. It will be most unusual if there are not a lot of them. At an appropriate moment towards the end of the discussion repeat the original mime.

Often during this discussion people will say, 'I thought you were doing something else', and this is an opportunity to make the point that when we see something that is unclear or ambiguous we try to make it fit our own preconceptions so that it makes sense to us. In this instance the preconceptions were suggested by the name of the game.

* Observers allow you to use this exercise with a group that is larger than 10. They are to note any additions to or omissions from the previous mime. This can be done on a form like the H3 **Listening chain** instruction sheet.

ESCAPE

Materials: Copies of the instruction sheets (pages 192–5).

Time: 1–1½ hours.

Procedure

1 Divide the participants into groups of between 6 and 10. Appoint an observer in each group who does not take part in the discussion. Distribute instruction sheets to all the group members and the observer instruction sheet to the appointed person.
2 Answer any questions about the procedure on the instruction sheet. Do not comment on the list of people or the information about them printed in normal typeface.
3 Give the group(s) 40 minutes to make their choices. You may wish to remind them of the time by giving them periodic warnings of the time, e.g. after 33 minutes say:

The 7 minute early warning system has just been sounded. The enemy missiles are on their way.

If any group finishes earlier than the others then you may wish to emphasize:

You will be in very cramped conditions in the rocket for a long time with very little opportunity for privacy. Are you sure of your choice?

4 After all the groups have reached a decision or the 40 minutes are over, bring the people back together into a single group.
   Ask the observers to outline what happened in their group.
   Use this as the basis for a discussion of:

- *how did you feel about this game?*
- *did anyone on the list arouse your prejudices?*
- *did you change your mind about any of the people in this game?*
- *did anyone persuade you to change your mind and if they did what did they say?*
- *if you met such people in everyday life how would you feel and behave?*

Variations

1 This game can also be used to emphasize the importance of thinking about the interviewer's needs in a job interview by changing the focus of the discussion.

Ask the observers to outline what happened in their group. Use this as a basis for a discussion of:

- *how do you feel about this game?*
- *why did you make the choices you did?*

The usual answers are (i) continuing the human race and (ii) the usefulness of that person to the group.

2 Tell them:

It has just been discovered there is less fuel than expected so fewer people can go. I now want each one of you to say briefly why you should be selected to go.

Don't ask probing or personal questions. Note how far each person gives an answer which addresses itself to the reasons used by the group for selecting people off the list.

3 Comment on how far the answers given satisfy the reasons for selecting the people off the list. It is not unusual to discover answers which don't satisfy these reasons, e.g. 'I am a nice person and make people laugh' or 'I am well liked.'

4 Ask them:

- *how far do your reasons for escaping match the groups criteria for selecting people from the list?*
  - *if this inteview had been for real do you think you would have got a place if you don't satisfy the main reasons behind the selection process?*
- *what are the implications for job interviews?*
- *what are the main things employers are looking for?*

L3 ESCAPE – INSTRUCTION SHEET

In 40 minutes the Earth is about to be totally destroyed. All the members of your group are safely inside a rocket which can escape this disaster. There is enough fuel and food for 30 years. You are travelling in the hope that you will find somewhere that is habitable but this is by no means certain. The accommodation is rather cramped and there is very little opportunity for privacy.

Your places on the rocket are safe and you cannot be asked to give them up. There are ten people outside the rocket who are hoping to escape and from these you must choose only five to fill the remaining places to balance the rocket for take off. You are the only people to escape from the world.

It is in everyone's interests that the group should make its decisions as unanimously as possible. You will be asked the reasons for your choices later.

1 Priest Aged 35 – white – previously a vet – a quiet person who is often able to calm and comfort others.

2 Pregnant woman Aged 25, and seven months pregnant – Pakistani – a good cook of Indian foods – she is in good health and expects a normal delivery – she is a practising Moslem.

3 Pregnant woman's husband Aged 26 – Pakistani – runs a successful building business and is competent in all the basic construction skills.

4 Armed policeman Aged 38 – white – awaiting promotion to Inspector – trained in the use of firearms and electronic communications – commended for bravery after rescuing two people from a burning car – leaving a wife and two children – carrying a loaded pistol.

5 Footballer Aged 22 – male – white – also trained as a butcher – well thought of as a footballer – has a knack of rallying the team when they seem demoralized or about to face defeat – also trained as a butcher.

6 **Nurse**   Aged 25 – male – white – qualified in both general medical and psychiatric nursing – gay – leaving behind a male companion with whom he has lived for the last five years – a regular attender of a Protestant church.

7 **Blonde actress**   Aged 22 – white – trained as a primary school teacher before becoming a successful actress in TV comedies – had a nervous breakdown four years ago.

8 **Geologist**   Aged 32 – female – white – has had two children by a previous marriage – now divorced – working for a mining company identifying rock specimens – has been actively involved with the Moonies.

9 **Science student**   Aged 20 – male – black – completed two years of a degree course in micro-electronics and the use of computers – parents are from the West Indies – he is interested in the Rastafarian beliefs and practices.

10 **Teenager**   Aged 14 – female – white – still at school and interested in sciences – tends to be moody which could just be her age but her parents had arranged for her to see a psychologist next week to get advice about this.

All ten people are physically and mentally fit unless stated otherwise.

L3 ESCAPE – OBSERVER INSTRUCTION SHEET

Time discussion started: ....

Decision made or changed about	Taken/left	Time	Main reasons given for choice
1			
2			
3			
4			
5			
6			
7			
8			
9			
10			
11			
12			

Did you see any examples of prejudice? Give examples.

What methods of reaching a decision were tried?

Did any of the people change their views because of the discussion?

SABOTEUR

Materials: Pencils and rubbers (several for each group). Instruction sheets and plans (pages 200–13), namely:

- General instruction sheets for everyone.
- Personal instructions for everyone except observers and timekeepers.
- Observer sheet.
- Timekeeper sheet.
- Maze plan (one for each group).
- Maze master copy.
- Maze solution.

Table for each group. Table for maze master copy, out of sight of the participants.

Time: 1–1½ hours.

Procedure

1 Out of sight of the group place a tick on all the *personal instructions* to indicate 'You are not a saboteur' and fold them over. Keep them in a safe place until they are distributed in procedure 5.
2 Arrange the room so that the *maze master copy* is placed out of sight of the groups behind a screen or outside the door. The *timekeeper instruction sheet* should also be placed here.
3 Each team will need a table which is not easily overlooked by the other teams or passed by them on the way to the *maze master copy*.
4 One person will need to act as a *timekeeper*. Divide the rest into groups of 5–8 people and ask one person on each table to act as the *observer*. The observers do not participate in solving the puzzle but still receive a copy of the *general instruction sheet* to inform them about the game.
5 Once everyone has settled down, distribute *general instruction sheets* to everyone. Tell the groups:

*In this game the aim is to complete the drawing of the maze that is in front of you so that it is the same as the **master copy** on the table over there.*

   Only one person at a time from any team may go to see the

master copy. *No notes can be made there nor can that person speak until he/she has returned and sat down. Every time someone goes to the* **master copy** *30 seconds are added to the time taken by the group in the second stage of the game. It does not matter if you spend more or less time than this looking at the master copy: you will still have 30 seconds added. The timekeeper will make sure you obey the rules while you are there and will record the number of visits by your team.*

Taking notes and speaking are allowed between the team members sitting at their table, and this will be recorded by the observer.

During this stage no one must draw any routes through the maze on the maze plan. Any team doing so will be disqualified.

You can have as long as you need to complete the maze. No penalties are added for being the slowest except for the number of visits to the **master copy.**

When you are satisfied that you have completed the **maze plan** *correctly you are to tell me. I cannot tell you if you are right. I will come over and time you while you draw out all the routes through the maze from A to B. This time will be added to the time recorded by the timekeeper and the team with the shortest time wins. If any of your routes are wrong I will continue to time you until you get it right; the timekeeper will continue to charge you 30 seconds for every visit to the* **master copy.**

However, there is a catch in this game. Just as in real life not everyone works towards the same goal or for the same reasons, this can also happen in games. I will give you each a set of **personal instructions** *which tells you whether or not you are a saboteur. Be careful not to show it to anyone in the group or to hold it so that the light shines through it allowing others to see what it says. After you have read it put it in a safe place, in your pocket or elsewhere; do not show it to anyone until the game is over.*

Distribute the *personal instructions* and give them time to read them:

If a group believe they know who the saboteur or saboteurs are they can stop them taking any further part in the game by everyone voting to say that person is a saboteur. The decision must be unanimous so everyone must agree. You will not know if you have made the right decision until the end of the game.

Do not over-explain. Make sure they know about the two stages. The rest will become clearer as they go along if they read their *general instructions*.

6 Run the game and calculate the times of each team. The team with the shortest time wins.

7 Start a discussion by asking the observer for each group to say, briefly:

- *how did the group try to solve the problem?*
- *did they work as a team?*
- *did the possibility of there being a saboteur concern them?*

Then widen the discussion to include everyone:

- *how much were you affected by being in competition with the other groups?*
- *how do you feel now that you know there were no saboteurs?*
- *if you decided there was a saboteur, what did they do to try to convince you that they were not?*
- *what effect did their attempts to deny being a saboteur have on you?*
- *how does the person that was thrown out feel?*
- *did you work better without that person?*
- *do you think this sort of situation ever arises in everyday life where people are wrongly accused or are used as an excuse for the difficulties other members of the group are having?*

Instruction sheets and mazes for playing L4 Saboteur are on pages 200–13.

Instructions for preparing the material
for L4 Saboteur

1 Photostat pages 208–13.
2 Join the box lines so that W meets X and Y meets Z.

L4 SABOTEUR – GENERAL INSTRUCTION SHEETS

This game is in two stages.

Stage one

1 The aim is to complete the *maze plan* so that it is the same as the *maze master copy*. You can take as long as you need over this stage, *but:*

2 You will be charged 30 seconds every time someone goes to see the *maze master copy* regardless of how long they spend there.

3 Only one person at a time from your group may go to look at the *maze master copy*. NB. *You are not allowed to take notes or to talk while you are away from the group until you have returned and sat down.*

4 You will each have been given personal instructions telling you whether or not you are a saboteur. You must not let anyone see these until after the game.

5 If you suspect someone is a saboteur you may challenge them. They can be thrown off the team and must take no further part in the game provided everyone else agrees and there is a unanimous vote about the identify of a saboteur. There may be more than one in any team. You cannot find out if you are right or wrong until the game is finished.

6 *You must not draw any routes through the maze until stage two. Any team that begins to draw any route in stage one will be banned from the game.*

7 When you are sure you have completed the *maze plan* so that it is the same as the *maze master copy*, signal for the leader to come over and time you for stage two. The leader cannot tell you if your completed maze is correct.

Stage two

1 Draw out all the possible routes through the maze from A to B. You will be timed while you do this and the routes will be checked.

2 If you make a mistake the timing continues until the correct solution is found. Your team is also charged 30 seconds for each visit to the *maze master copy*.

Total time

Number of visits =   × 30 seconds   =

Time for stage two   total time =

L4 SABOTEUR – PERSONAL INSTRUCTIONS

In real life not everyone in a group works towards the same goal. Some people may try to pursue their own aims because they do not like the group or its leader or due to a mistrust of the others. Sometimes it is because they have stronger ties with another group. In all these instances they sabotage the work of the group. There may be one or more saboteur(s) in your group. The tick in the box tells you which you are.

You are a saboteur   [   ]

You are not a saboteur   [   ]

If you are a saboteur you are to slow your team down but without giving yourself away.

If you are not a saboteur you are to help your team towards finding the solution as quickly as possible.

L4 SABOTEUR – OBSERVER SHEET

You are to take notes of what happens within your group. One of the simplest methods is to make a note of what is being said at 3 minute intervals and to add extra information about who seems to be the leader and note if this changes. As the game is about the fear of there being a saboteur in the group, note who is accused of being one and by whom.

Time	Observation

At the end of the game be prepared to say:

- *how did the group try to solve the problem?*
- *did they work as a team?*
- *did the possibility of there being a saboteur concern them?*

L4 SABOTEUR – TIMEKEEPER INSTRUCTION SHEET

You are to place a tick next to each team every time one of the members consults the *maze master copy*. For each tick they will add 30 seconds to their finishing time.

	NUMBER OF VISITS TO THE MAZE MASTER COPY	TOTAL
TEAM A		
TEAM B		
TEAM C		
TEAM D		
TEAM E		

- No more than one person at a time from each team may visit the *maze master copy*.

- Whoever visits the *maze master copy* is not allowed to speak or take notes until that person has gone back to his/her own group and is sitting down.

- When the game is over tell each team the number of visits it has made.

L4 SABOTEUR—MAZE PLAN

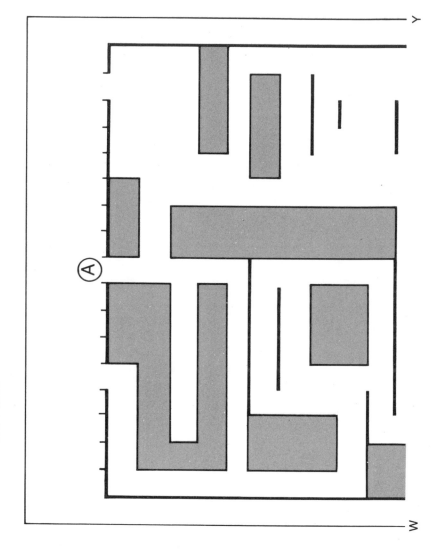

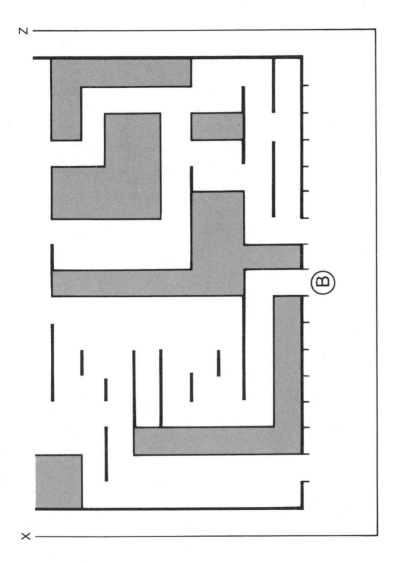

© Tim Bond 1985

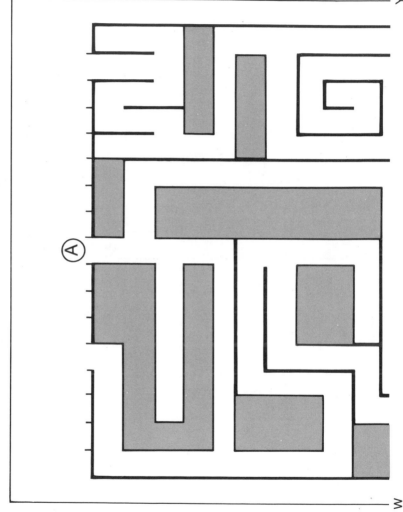

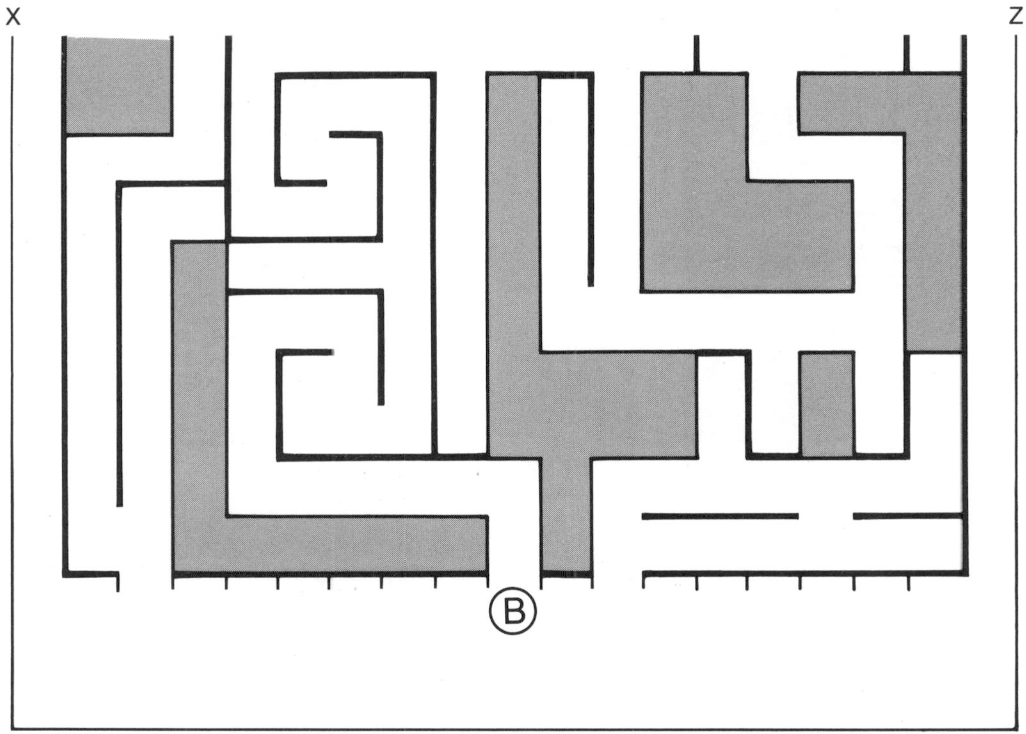
X
Z
B

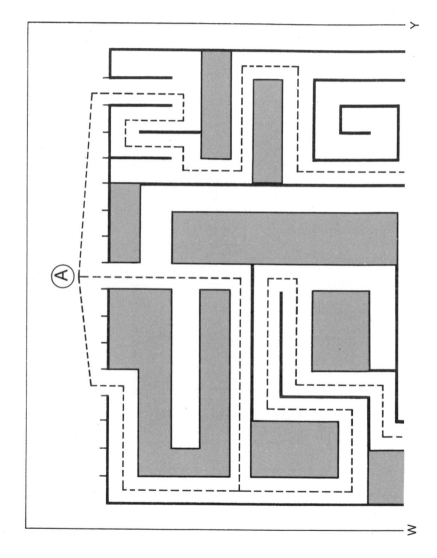

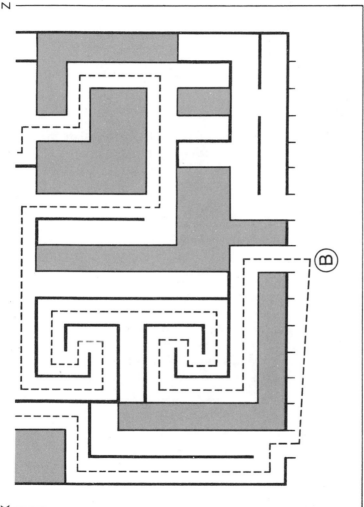

Sharing, negotiating and compromise

Aims
1 To provide experience in negotiating.
2 To introduce the idea that negotiation can be made easier by preparing a list of priorities beforehand.

General comments
Negotiating generally involves striking a balance between other people's needs and one's own needs so that whatever is agreed is acceptable to all parties. This increases the chance that any decisions that are agreed will last and will not be destroyed by someone's sense of grievance or being hard done by. The whole process can be made easier if all the parties come prepared with their own itemized list of priorities.

M1 **Squares** can be solved only by group cooperation and sharing.

M2 **Dream holiday** is the simplest of the exercises and looks at the process of ranking priorities.

M3 **Workmate** and M4 **Choosing a car** involve more complex procedures. Both start by asking individuals to prepare their own list of priorities as the basis for a subsequent negotiation. M3 **Workmate** can end here or in its variation go on to look at the influence of prejudice in this process.
M4 **Choosing a car** goes on to an additional negotiation for which the group has to make its own preparation and decide its own rules.

GAME	TIME	GROUP	MATERIALS
M1 SQUARES	20-30 minutes	Groups of 5	INSTRUCTION SHEET Five envelopes containing 18 pieces
M2 DREAM HOLIDAY	35 minutes	Pairs	Pens & copies of INSTRUCTION SHEETS
M3 WORKMATE	$1\frac{1}{4}$ hours	Groups of 5	Pens & copies of INSTRUCTION SHEET
M4 CHOOSING A CAR	$1\frac{1}{4}$ hours	Groups of 3 or 4	Pens & copies of the QUIZ Parts 1 & 2

SQUARES

Materials: Instruction sheets (page 217). Envelopes containing the 18 pieces which make up 5 squares (pages 218–19).

Time: 20–30 minutes.

Procedure

1 Sit five people around a table. It helps to prevent cheating if the table is large enough for them to be at least one arm's length from each other.
2 Distribute instruction sheets and envelopes. Answer questions to ensure they know the rules but do not interpret them or give additional information, e.g. number of pieces in each square.
3 After running the game discuss:

- *how did you communicate, as you were not allowed to talk or point?*
- *were you able to establish an agreed strategy or was control given to one or more members of the group?*
- *how frustrated did you become?*
- *at what point did you start to consider the need to break up established squares to find a total solution?*
- *did anyone resist or help this process?*
- *to what extent do problems within groups require attempts at overall solutions rather than attempts at solutions by one person or a minority of the group?*

M1 SQUARES – INSTRUCTION SHEET

1 You will be given an envelope containing parts of squares. Between you there are enough pieces to make up five squares of equal size.

2 The game is completed when the five squares have been constructed.

3 No single person may have more than five pieces in front of them at any one time.

4 *You must not take pieces from another player or signal for a piece to be given to you. You can only give pieces away.*

5 You must not talk or use sign language.

M1 SQUARES – MAKING THE PIECES

1 Cut the pieces out of five 6″ × 6″ cardboard squares.

   The problem can be made more difficult by using different coloured card provided no single square is made of the same coloured pieces.

2 Write the letters on both sides of each piece.

3 Label five envelopes A, B, C, D, E and put the pieces with the corresponding letter into that envelope.

   Envelopes A–C each contain 4 pieces.
   Envelopes D and E each contain 3 pieces.

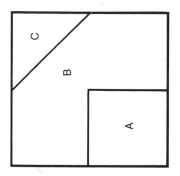

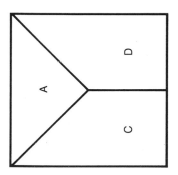

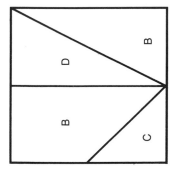

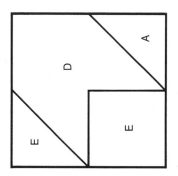

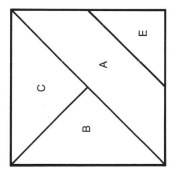

DREAM HOLIDAY

Materials: Pens and copies of instruction sheet (pages 222–3).

Time: 35 minutes.

Procedure

1 Distribute copies of instruction sheet and explain:

You are all the winners of a dream holiday for two. You have £5000 to spend on any holiday you like. In the box labelled 'DREAM HOLIDAY' write down where you would like to go, for how long, at what time of year and what you would like to do. Keep your answer to yourself at this stage.

Give them some minutes to do this.

2 Explain:

In box 2 you will see there is space for up to six reasons for your choice. Write down your main five or six reasons and then number them with the most important first and least important last. Keep your answer to yourself.

Give them about 5 minutes to do this.

3 Inform them:

That was the good news. The bad news is that the competition organizers have the right to decide who the other person you are going with is. I will now tell you who that person is . . .

Try to select people with different backgrounds and interests and move them into pairs.

You are to negotiate a holiday for two costing no more than £5000 which is acceptable to both of you.
    When you have done this complete the bottom box on the instruction sheet.

4 Bring them back into the large group – go round everybody asking them to say:

- where did they first dream of going and where did they end up?
- how far did their final choice satisfy the reasons for choosing the first destination?
- do they think the process of making a choice was made easier by having analysed the reason for their first choice? Was it easier than if they had just started with each person choosing a destination but giving no more details?

Variations

1 The game can be simplified by dividing them into pairs or threes and asking them to agree a description of one new addition to the team. The description must be realistic.
2 An alternative approach is to distribute the prepared descriptions of 5–6 people they must choose from. It is important that this list includes people from within the group's own age and interest range. They then make their selection and discuss points as in the original game.
3 If one of the aims is to highlight the influence of prejudice on negotiations then after the groups have followed your instructions in procedure 2 ask each group to letter their possible choices, including those not selected, A, B, C, etc. After they have done this inform them:

A – is the opposite sex.
B – is 5 years older (or younger).
C – is homosexual.
D – is a different colour.
E – is as described.
F – is handicapped (describe the handicap but it should not be one experienced by any of the group members).

Ask them to look at their choice of three people again and to reconsider their choices. The final discussion will be focussed on prejudice.

1

FIRST PRIZE

DREAM HOLIDAY FOR TWO COSTING UP TO £5000

Where do you want to go? . . . .

. . . .

For how long? . . . .   At what time of year? . . . .

What do you want to do? . . . .

. . . .

. . . .

2

DO NOT FILL IN THIS BOX UNTIL YOU ARE ASKED TO

Reasons

[   ] .... [   ] ....

[   ] .... [   ] ....

[   ] .... [   ] ....

3

DO NOT FILL IN THIS BOX UNTIL YOU ARE ASKED TO

Where are you going? ....

.... At what time of year? ....

For how long? ....

What will you both be doing? ....

....

....

WORKMATE

Materials: Pens and copies of instruction sheet.

Time: 1¼ hours.

Procedure

1 Distribute instruction sheet and give everyone 10–15 minutes to complete it. This may be done on their own, in which case they should not show their answers to anyone. In groups of 10 or more they may work in pairs and receive help from the other person. The pairs are then split up for the next stage of the game.

2 Divide them into groups of 5–7 and explain:

> *You are to imagine that each group will be working on its own for the next month with the same members as it has now, with three additional new members.*
>
> *One of the first tasks of your group is to select these three additional new members from the descriptions of your ideal workmate. Each one of these descriptions is a separate person and cannot be altered now.*
>
> *Each one of you in turn will describe your ideal workmate and give that person a name. The others may take notes on the back of their instruction sheets.*
>
> *The group may ask for information on the form to be clarified. This is O.K. but the writer should not add new information at this stage.*
>
> *When this process is completed in about 10 minutes, you have an additional 20 minutes to decide on who the three new additions to the team are. This decision must be one which everyone agrees with.*

3 Run the game and once all the groups have reached a decision or exceeded the time limit ask all the individual group members to look at the five most important characteristics they have chosen for a new workmate, and to tick them if they are satisfied by any of the three additional people. If any aspect is satisfied by two or three of the chosen people they are to give themselves the same number of additional ticks.

4 Bring the groups together for a discussion by:

- asking one member from each group to say what the main characteristics of the chosen people were;

and then open the discussion to everyone by asking:

- *how hard was it to reach a group decision?*
- *how many of your five original important points were satisfied?*
- *did you use these when you were trying to negotiate who would join the team and were they helpful?*

You may wish to point out that many professional negotiators prepare lists of the things they want to win in order of importance so that they know what they need to win and what can be given up in the interests of reaching an agreement.

Variations

1 The game can be simplified by dividing them into pairs or threes and asking them to agree a description of one new addition to the team. The description must be realistic.

2 An alternative approach is to distribute the prepared descriptions of 5–6 people they must choose from. It is important that this list includes people from within the group's own age and interest range. They then make their selection and discuss points as in the original game.

3 The game can also be used to show how prejudice distorts negotiations. After the groups have completed procedure 2 ask them to label each of the possible additions to their team A, B, C. This includes the descriptions of the people who were not selected. Inform them:

A – is the opposite sex.
B – is 5 years older (or younger)
C – is homosexual.
D – is a different colour.
E – is as described.
F – is handicapped (describe the handicap but it should not be one experienced by any of the group members).

Ask them to look at their choice of three people again and to reconsider their choices. The final discussion will be focussed on prejudice.

M3 WORKMATE – INSTRUCTION SHEET

Write down the characteristics of someone you would like to work with in your present situation doing the same sort of thing as you do now.

Sex: Male/Female   Age:

Personal qualities, e.g. willing to take orders, works well in a crisis, good looking, well mannered, funny, etc.

....

....

Qualifications: ....

....

....

Other interests/hobbies: ....

....

Invent a name for this person: ....

Once you have got as clear a picture as possible of this person write down the five most important things which make you want to work with him/her. After you have done this put numbers in the boxes with 1 for the most important thing to 5 for the least important.

[   ] . . . .

[   ] . . . .

[   ] . . . .

[   ] . . . .

[   ] . . . .

You may make notes on the back of this sheet during the rest of this game.

CHOOSING A CAR

Materials: Pens and copies of the quiz, parts 1 and 2 (pages 230–1). Car share rota sheets (pages 232–3).

Time: 1¼ hours.

Procedure

1 Distribute copies of the quiz part 1 to everyone and ask them to complete it in the next 10 minutes. They are to keep their answers to themselves at this stage.

2 Divide them into small groups of three or four and distribute copies of the quiz part 2 to everyone. Explain:

A rich benefactor has decided to donate one car to each group. However he has imposed two conditions which must be satisfied before the cars can be handed over.

The first is that the group unanimously agree on the five important features of the car as well as the type of car they want. You are to record the groups decisions on part 2 of the quiz which I will give you. You have 20 minutes to do this.

Distribute the quiz and when they have completed this stage explain.

The final condition is that the group must agree how they will share the use of the car for two weeks starting next Sunday. All the members of the group must agree to the car sharing rota which is part 3 of the quiz. So far as possible you should base your discussions on your real commitments over this fortnight. You have 20 minutes to do this.

Distribute part 3 of the quiz.

3 After they have completed both parts of the quiz bring them together to discuss:

- what type of car did each group select and what were its most important features? (Go quickly round the group.)
- how far did these match the features each of you identified as individuals? If they match up totally did you force your choice on the group? If they did not match up did you give in too easily?

- do you think having worked out your own order of importance for the features of the car helped the negotiations?
- did any group attempt to work out individual priorities before negotiating the rota? Would it have helped?
- what methods did you use to decide the rota? E.g. did you establish any rules to help in the decision making? How did you know everyone agreed?
- how do you feel about the decisions?
- would you do anything differently next time around?

M4 CHOOSING A CAR – QUIZ

Part 1

Read through the list of various features of cars. Underline the *five* features you would most like to have in a car of your own.

[ ] Bright colour
[ ] Causes the least pollution possible
[ ] Extra lights
[ ] Large luggage space
[ ] Latest braking system
[ ] Low maintenance costs
[ ] Modern design

[ ] Quiet
[ ] Rapid acceleration
[ ] Power steering
[ ] Strengthened to survive accidents
[ ] Soft top
[ ] Low petrol consumption
[ ] Vintage style
[ ] Wide wheels

After having underlined the five features you like best, number them in order of preference. Use 1 for the most important feature and continue down to 5 for the least important, e.g.

[*1*] Modern design

Number the types of car 1–4 according to your own choice, starting with 1 again, e.g. if you would most like to have a sports car [*1*] Sports car

[ ] Estate car
[ ] Family saloon

[ ] Rugged cross-country style
[ ] Sports car

Part 2

Imagine that a rich eccentric man has been pleased by a kindness your group has done for him. He is willing to buy your group one vehicle between you provided you can agree on its five most important features and the type of car. You must also agree on how you propose to share it.

Write down the five features you have agreed between you:

[ ] . . . . [ ] . . . .

[ ] . . . . [ ] . . . .

[ ] . . . .

Write down the type of car:

[ ] . . . .

Part 3

You must now decide on how to share out the use of the car over the fortnight starting next Sunday. If you cannot drive, you will be provided with a driver for your turn.

You must agree on a system of sharing the car which seems fair to all of you and then complete the rota sheets. Base it on your real commitments and plans for the next two weeks. Write your own times in, e.g.

| TUES | 8 ← John → 12 ← Sue → 2 ← Dave → 6 ← All out together → 12 |

M4 CHOOSING A CAR – CAR SHARE ROTA

Week 1

Day	Morning	Afternoon	Evening
Sun			
Mon			
Tues			
Wed			
Thurs			
Fri			
Sat			

Week 2

Day	Morning	Afternoon	Evening
Sun			
Mon			
Tues			
Wed			
Thurs			
Fri			
Sat			

Trust games

Aims

1 To introduce the need for physical touch between people and the pleasure it brings.
2 To develop trust within the group. In an atmosphere of physical trust people find it easier to talk more openly.

General comments

Trust games are often a useful means of ensuring a variety of activity in longer courses and provide relief from exclusively verbal games. If they are performed in a caring manner they usually create a group sense of well-being. However, as with all games it is important that there is an opportunity to discuss the experience afterwards; ideally the discussion should be at least as long as the activity. It ought to allow people to say what they feel about the experience, especially:

- *what did you like about this experience?*
- *what did you not like or find difficult?*
- *what would have made it better for you?*

Trust is most apparent when someone has placed themselves at risk in some way. This means that group members are vulnerable to emotional or physical hurt. The games have been ordered so that they begin with those which involve the vulnerability of allowing someone to invade your body space. They work towards games where there is an element of physical risk, e.g. falling over or being dropped. Where physical dangers are known to exist, these are indicated. Many of the exercises are not suitable for people with injured backs, necks or limbs.

In some games closing eyes is used as a gauge of how much trust someone is feeling. The exercise can be repeated until someone has enough trust to lose the urge to look. The use of blindfolds is discouraged because it deprives someone of this indicator of their feelings and reduces the safety of the game.

Other suitable games: O3.

GAME		TIME*	GROUP	MATERIALS
N1	GROUP BREATHING	10 minutes	Any size	None
N2	GROUP LAUGHTER	10 minutes	Any size	None
N3	HEAD TRUST	15 minutes	Pairs	None
N4	FACE TRUST	10 minutes	Pairs	None
N5	INTO THE MIDDLE AND OUT AGAIN	10 minutes	10 or more	None
N6	TANGLED HUMAN CHAIN	10-15 minutes	10 or more	None
N7	MOVING HUMAN CHAIN	10-15 minutes	6 or more	None
N8	KNEE SITTING	10 minutes	6 or more	None
N9	BACK SIT AND STAND	10 minutes	Pairs	None
N10	BACK LIFT	10 minutes	Pairs	None
N11	ARCHES	10 minutes	Pairs	None
N12	LEANING OUT	10 minutes	Pairs	None
N13	TRUST WALK	10-15 minutes	Pairs	None
N14	TRUST FALL	10-15 minutes	Threes	None
N15	TRUST ROLL - STANDING	20-30 minutes	Groups of 7 or more	None
N16	TRUST ROLL - SITTING	20-30 minutes	Groups of 7 or more	None
N17	LIFTING THE PERSON	15-30 minutes	Groups of 7 or more	None
N18	PASSING THE PERSON BACK	30 minutes	16 or more	None

* These times are only approximate as groups vary in the time they need to establish trust. The games should continue until this is achieved and discussed.

GROUP BREATHING

Procedure

1 The group lies down face up in a circle with their heads pointing to the centre. They hold hands and shut their eyes.

2 They are to try to breathe in and out at the same time as their neighbours. After a short while of attempting this, ask them to breathe in deeply and then let the air out slowly and to repeat this concentrating on breathing out. They are still to breathe in time with their neighbours. This game combines relaxation with developing a sense of group identity.

GROUP LAUGHTER

Procedure

1 Everyone lies on the floor in a long chain. Each person has their head on someone else's stomach.

2 One person starts laughing and it spreads up and down the human chain.

HEAD TRUST

Procedure

1 Working in pairs, one person lies face up on the floor and the other kneels at that person's head.
2 The kneeling person lifts the other's head up and down and then side to side. The other person tries to relax his/her neck muscles.
3 Repeat the process with roles reversed.

FACE TRUST

Procedure

1 Two people stand facing each other.
2 Both people shut their eyes and each in turn explores the other's face with their hands.

Variations

The group wanders amongst each other with their eyes shut. At an agreed signal they touch the person closest to them. Each in turn explores the other's face before guessing their name. The leader may have to guide some people towards each other.

INTO THE MIDDLE AND OUT AGAIN

Procedure

1 The group stands in a circle holding hands.
2 They all shut their eyes and move inwards as far as possible until they meet the others coming in from the other side. This is done as gently as possible.
3 With eyes still shut they move outwards to make as large a circle as possible.
4 Repeat the movements inwards and outwards several times.

TANGLED HUMAN CHAIN

Procedure

1 The group forms itself into a circle and holds hands.
2 Without losing hold they advance into the middle and form the tightest tangle possible by climbing over others' arms or passing under them.
3 After the tightest possible knot has been formed the process is reversed. Without losing hold of each other's hands they unravel the tangle and return to standing in a circle.

If the group is too vigorous there is the slight risk of sprained or twisted wrists or arms. Most people let go before this happens.

Variations

After forming the circle one person lets go of one hand and then leads the line back on itself, weaving in and out and under and over arms. This continues until no further tangling is possible and then the line tries to unravel without anyone letting go.

MOVING HUMAN CHAIN

Procedure

1 The group forms itself into a line all facing in the same direction. Each person places their arms around the waist of the person in front of them. They hold on tightly.

2 The line lowers itself to the ground without anyone letting go. The line tries to move forward by all moving their feet together and then their shoulders alternately.

3 The line stands up without breaking the chain.

KNEE SITTING

Procedure

1 Ten or more people stand in a tight circle. Each person stands facing the back of someone with their hands on that person's shoulders.

2 At an agreed signal everyone lowers him/herself to sit on the knees of the person behind them and then at an agreed signal they stand up again. Repeat this several times.

Collapses are likely.

BACK SIT AND STAND

Procedure

1 Two people stand back-to-back and link arms.
2 They try to sit down together by leaning on each other's back, and then try to stand up again.

BACK LIFT

Procedure

1 Two people stand back-to-back and link arms.
2 One person leans forward and lifts the other off the ground. They take turns in doing this.

ARCHES

Procedure

1 Two people stand with their feet together facing each other. They hold their arms straight out in front of them and move backwards until their fingertips just touch.

2 The two lean forward slightly until their palms are touching and try to find the balance point. If this is not found one of them falls face forward.

LEANING OUT

Procedure

1 Two people stand face to face with their feet together. Each person's feet should be just touching the other person's feet, toe to toe.

2 They link hands and lean backwards and try to find the balance point. They can sway sideways, carefully matching each other. If the balance point is lost one of them falls backwards.

TRUST WALK

Procedure

1 One person shuts their eyes and allows themselves to be guided around by another person avoiding people and other obstacles.
2 Reverse roles.

Variations

The leading may be done by holding hands, placing hands on the shoulders, the person with their eyes shut grasping an elbow of the other or with the guiding partner giving spoken directions.

TRUST FALL

Procedure

1 Three people stand in a line. Two face each other and the other faces the back of the middle person.
2 The middle person shuts their eyes and is gently rocked backwards and forwards in gradually increasing movements. The rockers need to remember that shutting eyes tends to exaggerate the sense of movement.
3 Every willing person has a turn at standing in the middle.

TRUST ROLL – STANDING

Procedure

1 At least six people stand in a circle facing inwards. A volunteer stands in the middle with eyes shut.

2 The volunteer is supported as he or she leans backwards and is then passed round the circle. The volunteer should relax totally.

TRUST ROLL – SITTING

Procedure

1 At least six people sit in a circle with their feet around the feet of a volunteer standing in the centre of the circle. The volunteer shuts his or her eyes.
2 The volunteer leans backwards and is supported with feet and hands and passed round the group.

LIFTING THE PERSON

Procedure

1 One volunteer lies face up on the ground with eyes shut.
2 At least six people kneel around him/her, place their hands under the person lying down and gently lift and lower him/her several times.
3 Each person who is willing to be lifted has a turn.

PASSING THE PERSON BACK

Procedure

1 At least 16 people pair off and stand in two lines facing each other.

2 Volunteers stand at the front of the line and are carefuly lifted and passed back over the heads of the line. This may be with their eyes shut or open. Once at the back of the line they take their turn in passing people backwards.

There is a risk of someone falling or being dropped.

Relaxing

Aims
1 To help groups relax after a demanding experience.
2 To introduce techniques which can be used in everyday life.

General comments
Often people complain of headaches and other tensions after participating in a sequence of games. Self-exploration and learning new skills can be stressful. These exercises can be used at the end of courses to relax the group members and remove symptoms of stress.

O1 **Ssh . . .** is a basic breathing exercise which has obvious applications for everyday life as well as in the group. O2 **Relax the muscles** involves tensing muscles and then gradually relaxing them; combined with appropriate breathing it is very effective. O3 **Unwind** is a variation of this requiring the participation of other members of the group.

O4 **Shake a leg** works differently by getting rid of tensions and frustrations through physical activity and a group yell.

O5 **Guided fantasy** encourages relaxation by taking people through a carefully planned day-dream.

GAME	TIME	GROUP	MATERIALS
O1 SSH ...	5 minutes	Any size	None
O2 RELAX THE MUSCLES	10-15 minutes	Any size	None
O3 UNWIND	30 minutes	Any size	None
O4 SHAKE A LEG	10 minutes	Any size	None
O5 GUIDED FANTASY	45 minutes	Any size	None

Other suitable games: N1

SSH . . .

Materials: None.

Time: 5 minutes.

Procedure

1 Ask everyone to find enough space to be able to bend forward without touching anybody.
2 Explain:

Stand upright in a relaxed manner. Let your arms hang loosely at your side. Take deep breaths slowly. Really fill your chest and your stomach.

Allow them to do this several times until everyone has the idea.

I want you to concentrate on breathing out slowly. To help with this, after we have filled our lungs with air I want you to bend forward slowly and try to touch the ground with your hands. As you do this I want you to breathe out through your mouth going 'ssh . . .'

Repeat this procedure several times.

Now stand upright with your hands hanging loosely at your side. You can shut your eyes if you want to. Breathe in slowly and deeply and then release the breath slowly. Repeat this process concentrating on breathing out. Do this for 2 minutes.

3 Breathing slowly and deeply is one of the basic techniques that anyone can use to relax in a difficult situation. It can be used in almost any situation and if necessary in the presence of others. It is a technique which can be used before an important public event or an interview if you wish to calm your nerves.

Variations

The final 2 minutes of breathing slowly can be done lying down.

RELAX THE MUSCLES

Materials: None.

Time: 10–15 minutes.

Procedure

1 Ask everyone to lie on their back on the floor with their eyes shut. Say:

I am going to work through your main groups of muscles and ask you to tense them. Make them as hard and as tense as you can in your feet* ... your calves ... your thighs ... your buttocks ... your stomach ... your back ... your hands ... your arms ... your shoulders ... your neck ... your face ... including your tongue ....

2 Ask them to hold this position for about 30 seconds. Then say:

Now I want you to relax your muscles as I tell you to.
I want you to relax the muscles in your feet* ... let them go limp ... in your calves ... in your thighs ... in your buttocks ... in your stomach ... in your back ... the muscles in your hands ... in your arms ... in your shoulders ... in your neck ... in your face ... feel the muscles relax in your forehead ... your eyes ... your mouth ... your tongue.
Just breathe slowly. Concentrate on breathing out.

3 Allow them to continue in this state for a couple of minutes. Then say:

Now that you are all feeling relaxed I would like you to open your eyes and sit up slowly. Don't hurry. Just come back in your own time and sit up.

4 If anyone has fallen asleep they can be woken gently by rubbing their arms and legs, or can be left to sleep for some time.

This exercise is useful for anyone who suffers from sleeplessness. The process can be repeated on one's own at night. After relaxing fully, concentrate on *breathing* out slowly and sleep will usually follow.

* Pause for a few seconds to allow people to do it and experience the sensation. Do this every time there is a line of dots. The temptation is to press on too quickly.

UNWIND

Materials: None.

Time: 30 minutes.

Procedure

1 Divide the group into two with equal numbers in each part.
2 Half the group moves into the middle of the room. Each person will need enough space to lie down and have someone move around them without disturbing anyone else. Explain:

When you have found plenty of room you are to sit or crouch and using your legs and arms to tie yourself into a knot. When you have done this shut your eyes and try not to open them again until I tell you to. Someone will come and try to unravel you and lay you out in a comfortable position. You should try to resist their attempts to untie you for a short while until you feel ready to be untied.

3 Explain to the other half who have been standing watching this procedure:

You are each to select a person and to unravel them carefully so that they end up lying on the floor in a comfortable position. Be careful not to let them fall down. When your person is lying down arrange their limbs so that they are comfortable. Spend a few moments stroking the forehead or the back of the neck depending which way they are lying. The aim is to help the other person relax.

4 When this procedure has been completed ask the people doing the unravelling to return to the side of the room quietly. Leave the people on the floor lying down for a few minutes before asking them to open their eyes and sit up in their own time.
5 Ask the people sitting on the floor:

● *how did you find the experience?*
● *what was most pleasant or relaxing?*
● *is there anything that could have been done to make it more relaxing?*

6 Repeat the procedure with the groups reversing roles.

Variations

After the group doing the unravelling has moved back to the side of the room ask the people to concentrate on their breathing. They are to breathe slowly and concentrate on breathing out.

SHAKE A LEG

Materials: None.

Time: 10 minutes.

Procedure

1 Ask everyone to find enough space to be able to swing their arms without hitting anyone.
2 Explain:

I want you to hold your right arm out in front of you and shake the hand using the wrist* . . . now swing the arm from the shoulder . . . and rotate it like a windmill . . . and now the other way . . . Let it hang loose.

Now hold your left arm out in front of you and shake the hand using the wrist . . . now swing the arm from the shoulder . . . and rotate it again . . . and now the other way . . . Let it hang loose.

Lift your right leg off the ground and when you are balanced flap the foot using your ankle . . . now kick the leg backwards and forwards vigorously . . . and now rotate it from the hip . . . Let it hang loose . . . and stand on it.

Now lift your left leg and when you are balanced flap the foot using your ankle . . . now kick the leg backwards and forwards vigorously . . . Let it hang down loosely and stand on it.

Lift up whichever leg you want to . . . the one that feels most comfortable. I want you to imagine a large is holding your ankle and you are trying to shake it off . . . Give this a try and as you do this, I want you to shout 'Off, off' as loudly as you can.

The leader will need to start the shouting and it may need repeating several times until the group is really shouting vigorously.

Variations

Introduce shaking the dog off and shouting at the end of each leg shaking.

---

* Pause at the dots long enough to allow the activity to take place.

GUIDED FANTASY

Materials: One copy of the guided fantasy script (pages 261–4).

Time: 45 minutes.

Procedure

1 If possible arrange the room so that it is free of bright lights or sunshine.
2 Ask the group to take comfortable relaxed positions either lying on the floor or sitting in a chair with their head supported.
3 When they have all settled down start to read the script in a slow even voice pausing at the dots. It should take about 20 minutes. Some people find it helpful to deepen or soften their voice slightly as they read the passage.
4 After reading the passage give them time to open their eyes and start moving. Sometimes someone will have fallen asleep. They can either be left sleeping or can be woken by gently rubbing their hands and arms. Avoid waking them by sudden movements or loud noises.
5 Start a discussion about the experience by asking:

- *What parts of the guided fantasy were real to you?*
- *What did you enjoy most?*
- *Were there any bits you did not like?*
- *How did you feel in the forest?*
- *Did you go down the wire slide?*
- *What was your pleasurable find on the walk down the valley?*
- *Did you go into the glass-bottomed room?*
- *Where was your safe and comfortable place?*

Do not press the questions too hard or force answers from people, as some of the experiences may have been very personal.

O5 GUIDED FANTASY SCRIPT

I want you to close your eyes and relax . . . Make yourself comfortable . . .
Feel the way your body touches the floor or chair . . . Listen to the sounds
around you . . . Let them fade into the background . . . Breathe slowly . . .
and concentrate on breathing out.

We are all going on a journey in our imaginations . . . Try to picture the
scenes and events I describe . . . I will occasionally ask you questions . . .
Try to answer them in your own mind . . . We can discuss these and the
whole experience later . . .

Make sure you are comfortable and concentrate on breathing out
slowly . . . We are now ready to begin the journey.

It is dawn and we are all standing outside a railway station . . . You can
hear the train that brought us here pulling out and gradually moving into
the distance . . . In the half-light of dawn you can see before you forests
and mountains . . . A guide has come to meet us. He seems strong and
reliable . . . He is saying that he has planned a day which will be full of
adventure and excitement . . . There will be risks and it may be uncom-
fortable at times . . . You can choose not to go with him or to opt out later at
various stages in the journey . . . Do you want to go? . . . Does someone
encourage you? . . . or do you encourage someone to go?

The guide sets off through a small gate on to a forest path. The path is
narrow and everyone walks in single file. The guide explains that it is a big
forest and that if you leave the path it is easy to get lost. It looks very dark
under the trees . . . One bit of forest looks much like another bit of
forest . . . The path starts to twist and turn a lot so that you cannot always
see the people in front of you . . . Do you try to hurry to catch up? Do you
just keep moving at the same pace knowing that they will reappear when
you are round the bend? . . . You keep on walking for some time, often
bending down to go under branches.

Suddenly you come to the edge of the forest and the others in front of you
are sitting in a small hollow in the sunlight . . . The sun is just beginning to
warm the ground and the air . . . You lie down and look at the sky and the
clouds . . . How do you feel? . . .

You become aware of the sound of a river in the distance . . . The guide explains that just over the rise is a large gorge and that this can be crossed in two ways. It is possible to take a pleasant walk of a couple of miles and cross the river by a bridge . . . The other way is to cross on a wire slide. This involves weaving a safety harness and hanging by your hands from a pulley which races down from the cliff top to the edge of the water on the far side. There are people already waiting to catch you and help you on to the rocks. The choice is yours . . . Which do you choose? . . . Do you help anyone to make up their mind? . . . Does anyone help you to make up your mind? . . .

Those of you who decide to walk round to the other side enjoy a pleasant stroll through spring flowers and spectacular views. You arrive in time to see some of the others came down the wire slide.

Some of you decide to try the wire slide . . . You are strapped into a safety harness before you reach up to get hold of the bar and move to the cliff edge . . . You can hear the roar of the water which is white with foam as it races over the rapids. The far side is quieter but seems a long way down . . . Hanging on the bar you jump off the cliff and seem to drop several feet before the wire takes your weight and then you start to speed forwards . . . You can see the white water twisting and tumbling beneath you. The air whistles in your clothes and hair as you speed downwards . . . Do you shut your eyes? . . . Do you cry out? . . . As you come to the bottom the slide begins to slow and you can see the water is quieter here. You can either lift your legs clear of the water or let them touch the water and send spray arching away from you on either side . . . Which do you do? . . . Strong arms reach out and catch you and lift you on to the bank. As you sit down on a rocky ledge to watch the others come down, how do you feel? . . . What is your heart doing? . . . How do your arms and legs feel? . . . What do you think about? . . .

Gradually the group reassembles until you are all together again at the bottom of the gorge. The guide tells you he is going to take you along an old miner's track past the rapids. You move off in single file . . . The roar of the water becomes louder . . . It is impossible to make yourself heard above the noise . . . The spray from the rapids wets the rocks and heightens their colour . . . In the sunlight they glisten and are pleasant to touch . . . You see the person in front of you doing the same . . . Who is it? . . . Your eyes meet briefly . . . What do they communicate? . . . How do you respond? . . .

The path turns and moves back in the shadows of the overhanging cliffs . . . A little way ahead you can see a patch of sunlight and in it you see something which really pleases you. You approach and feel real pleasure . . . What is it you have seen? . . . You spend some moments there enjoying your find . . . The time has come to move on. You may leave your find there or may bring it with you. What do you do? . . . The rocky path continues to wind in and out of the sunlight.

Slowly the river banks become less steep and there is more grass and banks of flowers. The sound of the river is gentler now and you can see a comfortable old launch moored on its banks. As you climb aboard you can feel it moving gently on the water . . . The water is clear and flowing slowly . . . The mooring ropes are pulled in and the boat sets off slowly and moves round the bend in the river into a large lake . . . The lake is surrounded by trees and mountains and has several small islands . . . As the boat moves between these islands it gives you a good view of them and the birds and animals on them . . . The guide tells you the boat has a glass bottom and if you want you can go down below and see the lake bottom . . . Do you go?

If you want to you can climb down wooden stairs into a dimly lit room. You realize the blue-grey light is coming from the floor and not the ceiling. As you stand on it you realize the floor is glass and the light is from the sun passing through the water and into the room. Not far below you can see plants waving and fish swimming amongst them. You sit down and watch . . . It is as though you are part of that underwater world . . . What do you feel? . . . The boat's rocking and the movement of the water plants seem to merge as you watch the sun playing on the bed of the lake . . .

After a while you climb back to the deck and find the boat is approaching a small jetty. You are told this is not far from your starting point, but before you have to go back you can spend some time in a place of your choosing . . . There are many different places within easy walking distance of the jetty. You choose one which feels good to you . . . It is somewhere safe and comfortable . . . Where is it? . . . You look around and enjoy familiar objects you are fond of . . . What are they? . . . As you stay there you think of the experiences of the day . . . What did you enjoy the most? . . . Are you pleased you came? . . .

The guide comes to tell you it is time to return and in the sunshine you walk back to the station. The woods move gently in the breeze and the mountaintops seem hazy in the warm summer light . . . The train is standing waiting for you to bring you back . . . In your own time open your eyes . . . and when you are ready, sit up slowly.

Endgames

Aims

1 To provide a method of finishing the group's time together.
2 To allow feedback about the shared experience of members of the group.

General comments

A course ends naturally if the last activity (before goodbye) is a personal review of either the members' own progress or of the group relationships or of the course itself. This information is useful not only to course members but also to the leader for planning future courses.

P1 **Positive strokes** encourages pleasant feedback between group members and usually ends the course on a high note. P2 **While we have been together** combines personal feedback with feedback about the course in a non-threatening way.

P3 **Achievements** provides an opportunity for reviewing progress and planning the next goals in a personally chosen programme.

P4 **Resent/appreciate** is a widely used game to end courses because it is almost always successful. It also provides leaders with useful information about how the course has gone. P5 **Reflections** is a more open-ended way of reviewing the group experience.

GAME	TIME	GROUP	MATERIALS
P1 POSITIVE STROKES	About 2 minutes per person	Any size	None
P2 WHILE WE HAVE BEEN TOGETHER	About 3-4 minutes per person	Any size	Copies of prepared cards
P3 ACHIEVEMENTS	30-40 minutes	Groups of 3-5	Blackboard/ flipchart
P4 RESENT APPRECIATE	About 2-3 minutes per person	Any size	None
P5 REFLECTIONS	About 2-3 minutes per person	Any size	None

POSITIVE STROKES

Materials: None.

Time: About 2 minutes per person.

Procedure

1 Sit the group in a circle and explain:

   Most of us find it easier to say what is wrong with others and are slightly embarrassed to say what we like. Psychologists believe that all this criticism or negative strokes can lead to a poor image of ourselves and can in extreme cases help to cause mental illness. They believe we all feel much better if we also receive good, positive, accurate messages about ourselves. This is a game where we practise giving honest praise or positive strokes to our neighbour.

   Each of us will say something we like about our neighbour on the left. It must be honest and it must be something they do or something they can control. I will start the process.

   The thing I like about . . . (name of person on left) is . . .

2 The leader's contribution is important as it sets the standard for the others. E.g.

   'The thing I like about Alan is the way he is so calm even under pressure. When . . . happened he not only coped without getting angry or flustered but he . . .'

   is much better than *'The thing I like about Alan is his calmness'* as it explains what he does or doesn't do and in what circumstances.

3 Continue round the group. If they have not done this before you may be surprised at their slight embarrassment; this shows how ill at ease we are at praising each other and how much practice at it is needed. It is one way of ending a course on a high note.

WHILE WE HAVE BEEN TOGETHER

Materials: Copies of prepared cards (see page 269).

Time: About 3–4 minutes per person.

Procedure

1 Arrange the group in a circle. Place the cards in a pile face down in the centre.
2 Each person takes a card in turn and answers the question as honestly as they can. The question applies only to the time the group have been together for the course. If anyone is not sure how to word their answers they can begin it:

'While we have been together . . .'

If the group know each other well then any answer which is less than the truth will be seen for what it is.
3 After each person has spoken as prompted by their card, the others can ask questions to check points that are not clear.
4 Pass on to the next person until everyone has had a turn.

EXAMPLES FOR CARDS

While we have been together:

- the thing that made me most angry was. . .
- the funniest thing was. . .
- the thing I regret most. . .
- I was upset when. . .
- the most interesting thing was. . .
- the person who was kindest to me. . .
- the thing which made me most nervous was. . .
- the most valuable experience was. . .
- my best memory is. . .
- the person I wish I had got to know better. . .
- the thing I would most like to repeat. . .
- the thing which interested me least. . .
- the thing which made me angry with myself was. . .
- the thing I most disliked. . .
- the thing which frustrated me was. . .
- the thing I would like to do more of. . .
- the thing I would like to do less of. . .
- the thing that made me happy was. . .
- the person who has been a good friend. . .

ACHIEVEMENTS

Materials: Blackboard or flipchart to display questions.

Time: 30–40 minutes.

Procedure
1 Divide into groups of 3 to 5.
2 Ask them to take turns in discussing:

- *what did I hope to achieve when I began this course?*
- *what do I feel I have achieved in the course?*
- *what will I try to do differently because of the course?*
- *what do I plan to do next to build on the course or satisfy unmet needs?*

They are to help each other with the last two questions. The aim is that each person can see the practical implications of the course for themselves and they plan what they will do next to follow it up. This may include promising to tell a friend in a week's or a month's time how they feel the course has affected them, or how they have achieved a personal goal, or deciding to attend other courses.
3 The leader can circulate to help the discussions and if necessary ask the groups to come back into the large group and summarize their discussions and conclusions.

RESENT/APPRECIATE

Materials: None.

Time: About 2–3 minutes per person.

Procedure

1 Arrange the group so that they are sitting in a circle and introduce the game by saying:

We have all been through a range of experiences together. There will be some things we have liked and some things we have disliked. This is an opportunity to look at these. Each one of us will think about our experiences together and then make short statements beginning with the words:

'I resent . . . .' and 'I appreciate . . . .'

Try to be as honest as you can.

2 The leader starts the game and sets its tone. After a successful course, lack of time or distractions are often regretted; the company and quality of group members are appreciated. It is important that what is said is honest.
3 Work round the group clockwise giving everyone a turn.
4 The leader thanks the group for their comments and may choose to explore some of these further in a general discussion.

Variations

The wording can be changed, e.g.

'I did not like . . . .'; 'I liked . . . .'

REFLECTIONS

Materials: None.

Time: About 2–3 minutes per person.

Procedure

1 Sit the group in the circle and explain:

This is your opportunity to say what your strongest impression of the time we have spent together is. I want each of you in turn to imagine you are driving away in a car and you look back in the mirror and see this course. What is the strongest image you see reflected in the mirror? It can be a feeling or an event. After you have spoken the others can ask questions about what you have said.

2 Work round the group in turn or let people respond when they are ready until everyone has had a turn.

Review quiz

Aims

To provide someone with the opportunity to look back over a course to record personal goals for future reference.

General comments

This quiz is intended as a personal record to be completed at the end of a game/sequence of games so that someone can record their achievements and future goals. This could well be given out as homework or could be completed at the end of the course just before the endgame and goodbye.

Participants should be reminded to set goals they can achieve. Nothing succeeds like success; so if they set themselves goals and then achieve them they will be encouraged to try new goals.

QUIZ	TIME	GROUP	MATERIALS
Q1 REVIEW QUIZ	Varies according to number of the games used	Any size	Pens and copies of the quiz

REVIEW QUIZ

Game quiz	What I found I could do or things that were useful	What I need to do more of	What I will do next*

Say what you will do, how you will do it and by when. Remember to keep your goals realistic. If you can achieve them this will encourage you to attempt more.

Games for Social and Life Skills Tim Bond (Hutchinson 1985) © Tim Bond 1985

Useful books

COLLECTIONS OF GAMES/EXERCISES/SIMULATIONS

Donna Brandes and Howard Phillips, *Gamesters' Handbook,* Stanley Thornes (Publishers) Ltd (UK) 1979

Donna Brandes, *Gamesters' Two,* Stanley Thornes (Publishers) Ltd (UK) 1982

Jack Canfield and Harold Wells, *100 ways to enhance self-concept in the classroom*, Prentice Hall Inc., Englewood Cliffs (USA) 1976

Alec Davison and Peter Gordon, *Games and Simulations in Action*, Woburn Press (UK and USA) 1978

Daphne Lennox, *Residential Group Therapy for Children*, Tavistock Publications (UK and USA) 1982

J. William Pfeiffer and John E. Jones, *A Handbook of Structured Experiences for Human Relations Training*, Vols. 1–9, University Associates (USA) 1974–83

Louis Thayer, *Affective Education*, University Associates (USA) 1976

COUNSELLING SKILLS

Gerard Egan, *The Skilled Helper*, Brooks/Cole Publishing Co. (USA) 1975

E. A. Munro, R. J. Manthei and J. J. Small, *Counselling – A Skills Approach*, Methuen (NZ) 1979

Richard Nelson Jones, *Practical Counselling Skills*, Holt, Rinehart & Winston (UK) 1983

Philip Priestley and James McGuire, *Learning to Help*, Tavistock Publications (UK and USA) 1983

GROUPS AND WAYS OF WORKING WITH THEM

Tom Douglas, *Basic Groupwork*, Tavistock Publications (UK and USA) 1978

John Hodge, *Planning for Co-leadership – a practical guide for group workers*, Groupvine (UK), 43 Fern Avenue, Newcastle-upon-Tyne 1985

Fred Milson, *An Introduction to Group Work Skill*, Routledge & Kegan Paul (UK and USA) 1973

Ernest Stech and Sharon Ratcliffe, *Working in Groups*, National Textbook Company (USA) 1977

Leadership style
R. White and R. Lippitt, *Autocracy and Democracy*, Harper & Row (USA) 1960

Value of discussion
K. Lewin, 'Group decision and social change' in Maccoby, Newcomb and Hartley, *Readings in Social Psychology*, Holt, Rinehart & Winston (USA) 1958

LIFESKILLS

Clive Fletcher, *Facing the Interview*, Unwin Paperbacks (UK) 1981

Barrie Hopson and Mike Scally, *Lifeskills Teaching*, McGraw-Hill (UK) 1981

Barrie Hopson and Mike Scally, *Lifeskills Teaching Programmes*, Lifeskills Associates (UK) 1979

Chris Webb, *Communication Skills Talk Yourself into a Job*, Papermac (UK) 1979

NON-VERBAL COMMUNICATION

Michael Argyle, *Bodily Communication*, Methuen University Paperbacks (UK and USA) 1975

Desmond Morris, *Manwatching*, Triad Panther (UK) 1977

SOCIAL SKILLS TRAINING

Michael Argyle, *Social Skills and Health*, Methuen University Paperbacks (UK and USA) 1981

Michael Argyle, *Social Skills and Work*, Methuen University Paperbacks (UK and USA) 1981

Michael Argyle and others, *Social Skills and Mental Health*, Methuen University Paperbacks (UK and USA) 1978

Philip Priestly, James McGuire and others, *Social Skills and Personal Problem Solving*, Tavistock Publications (UK and USA) 1978

Philip Priestly, James McGuire and others, *Social Skills in Prison and the Community*, Routledge & Kegan Paul (UK and USA) 1984

Index

The names of games and section headings are in **bold**.